WHA... ...RD?
VOCABULARY ...PMENT IN
MULTILING...AL CLASSROOMS

WHAT'S IN A WORD?
vocabulary development in multilingual classrooms

Norah McWilliam

— I'M SO HUNGRY I COULD EAT A HORSE.
— YOU'RE KIDDING AREN'T YOU?

Trentham Books

First published in 1998 by Trentham Books Limited

Trentham Books Limited
Westview House
734 London Road
Oakhill
Stoke on Trent
Staffordshire
England ST4 5NP

British Cataloguing in Publication Data
A catalogue record for this book is available from the British Library
ISBN 1 85856 088 8

Designed and typeset by Trentham Print Design Ltd., Chester and
printed in Great Britain by The Cromwell Press Ltd., Wiltshire

Contents

ILLUSTRATIONS

The author wishes to thank Georgia Woollard for the illustration on the back cover and page iii and for the two drawings on page 146 and page 180. Thanks are also due to teachers and children whose work is illustrated throughout the book. Special thanks to Maggie Power and her pupils for their wonderful pieces, and to Yasmin of Manningham Middle School for her poem on page 79. Unless otherwise stated photographs are by the author. Photographs which feature advertisement copy have been taken of publicly displayed hoardings during the past five years. In each case the origin of the image is attributable to the manufacturing company of the product/service concerned and permission has been sought or obtained, as for other source material as follows: Fort Sterling Ltd. for 'Nouvelle Tissues' on page 3; kind permission of Nestlé Cereal Partners UK for 'Fruitful from Shredded Wheat' on page 18; kind permission of The Ryvita Company for 'Crackerbread' on page 20; kind permission of Yorkshire Bank for pages 27 and 159; The Children's Society for the picture on page 28; Ward Locke Educational for the extract by Joan Tough on page 40; kind permission of IBM Corporation for page 47; Addison Wesley-Longman Ltd. for permission to reprint extracts from the Longman Contemporary English Dictionary on pages 58 &144 ; Carling Brewing Company and kind permission of Ford of Europe Inc. for adverts on page 70; British Telecom for pages 77 & 78; Carlsberg for page 122; The Dalesman Magazine for the 'Proposal of Marriage' on page 135; teachers participants in Word-Weaving courses for pages 139 & 140; kind permission of Colgate-Palmolive for page 150; kind permission of Imperial Tobacco Ltd. for the Embassy Mild advertisement on page 155; Vodafone Ltd. for the People's Telephone advert on page 155; kind permission of Barclay's Bank for page 160; kind permission of Perrier Vittel UK. Ltd. for the advert on page 166; Pedigree Petfoods for the Whiskas catfood advert on page 167; kind permission from Dairy Crest Ltd. for the Clover advert on page 167.

page 3: Original image acknowledged

page 6: Permission sought from the National Canine Defence League

page 20: Original image acknowledged

page 27: Original image acknowledged

page 28: Original image acknowledged

page 47: Original image acknowledged

page 58: Longman Contemporary English Dictionary. Reprinted by permission of Addison Wesley-Longman Ltd.

page 70: Original images acknowledged

page 77: Original image acknowledged

page 78: Original image acknowledged

page 79: Yasmin, Manningham Middle School, 1996

page 117: Originator unknown

page 122: Original images acknowledged

page 139: With thanks to teachers participating in the in-service course 'Word-Weaving' 1996

page 140: With thanks to teachers participating in the in-service course 'Word-Weaving' 1996

page 143: Source: Sinclair (19787) Looking Up: an account of the COBUILD Project in lexical computing.

page 144: Longman Contemporary English Dictionary. Reprinted by permission of Addison Wesley-Longman Ltd.

page 146: Drawing by Georgia Woollard

page 149: Original image acknowledged

page 150: Original image acknowledged

page 152: Thankyou, Maggie Power and children of Grange Road First School

page 155: Original images acknowledged

page 156: With thanks to teachers participating in the in-service course 'Word-Weaving' 1996

page 161: Original images acknowledged

page 163: Source: Reader's Digest Reverse Dictionary

page 166: Original image acknowledged

Page 167: Original images acknowledged

Page 175: Thankyou Maggie Power and children of Grange Road First School.

Page 176: With thanks to teachers participating in the in-service course 'Word-Weaving' 1996

Page 180: Drawing by Georgia Woollard

DEDICATION

To Mary Buckley
who lived indomitably
from 1912 to 1997
and who got me started.

And to Georgia, Thomas and Charlotte
who live awesomely
and let me get on with it.

ACKNOWLEDGEMENTS

The ideas in this book arise out of years of dialogue in the Department of Teacher Education, Bradford and Ilkley College among members of the Language and Literature Strand whose involvement in multilingual classrooms continues, in spite of everything, to be imaginative, energetic and insightful. I am grateful to them all for their personal and professional skills and generosities. Many students and teachers whom I have met in classrooms over the years have also stimulated ideas and provided examples which I have drawn on. In addition, the collective wisdom and wit of many individuals has helped me to shape ideas over time, though they may not know it and may not altogether agree with the outcome: particularly Stanislaw Dylak, Audrey Gregory, Amrik Kalsi, Amar Khela, Savitri Pema, Maggie Power and Robin Richardson. Of all theorists, I must acknowledge the influence of Jim Cummins, whose commitment to the empowerment of bilingual children is internationally admired.

Above all I am indebted to Barré Fitzpatrick, whose understated clemency as creative thinker and perceptive researcher made him the critical friend I needed to pull the book together. The errors and shortcomings of the book are entirely my own.

Introduction

This book is chiefly for teachers (and students in initial teacher-education) who are working with children in multilingual UK classrooms. All our classrooms are actually or potentially multilingual and the sooner they are all actually so, the better. *All* our children need the cognitive and cultural enrichment that multilingualism endows and so do all teachers. English is certainly a language which huge numbers of people all over the world consider to be a means of extending cultural, professional and commercial opportunities, but if this is gained to the detriment of cultural and cognitive use of other languages, our shared future will be the poorer for it.

In speaking to teachers I am not speaking to two separate groups: those who do and those who do not share the linguistic repertoires of their pupils. This would be an anachronism which ignores the complexity of individual and collective linguistic experience in the UK and in all linguistically diverse milieux. I work in a department of teacher-education with colleagues whose knowledge of language, i.e. language *per se*, far exceeds the boundaries of the collected words and sounds we call 'English'. We work with students whose ranges of cultural and linguistic experience are ever-changing – as are ours. Many of our students initially describe themselves as 'English monolinguals', as though this is a fact which defines their identity for all time. Their active use of different languages may indeed be very limited, but we see it as a vital part of our roles as tutors in language education to try to persuade them that these limitations can be whittled away by gradually and determinedly taking on the task of activating their passive knowledge of other languages and by learning about English in ways which equip them to pass on a powerful set of skills to the children they will teach. Some of the students we work with have used a language other than English from early childhood and bring to their intended profession a linguistic treasure-trove which is waiting to be shared with all children. Not all see it quite like that: many of them are conscious that their oracy and literacy skills in 'first language' are limited in ways which inhibit their professional and academic confidence and prevent them from utilising their bilingualism for the benefit of the children they will teach. They too need to attend to the limiting factors of their language repertoire.

There is no clear-cut division between teachers who share children's linguistic and cultural experiences and those who do not. There can never be a precise match between the linguistic and cultural experiences of a teacher and the linguistic and cultural experiences of a whole class of children, even when they appear to 'belong' to a shared linguistic and cultural heritage. Common sense tells us that age, gender and social 'class' create important differences between teachers and pupils, let alone ethnicity and individual personality.

Classrooms in the UK are affected, as in all countries, by children's immersion in international communications technology and by their families' mobility between countries. Whilst English will continue to dominate and serve us all as a uniting and empowering lingua franca, the geographical land-mass we call the UK has always housed a multilingual population whose allegiances to different languages and dialects have been a driving force in drawing and re-drawing political boundaries through the centuries. That diversity is increasingly more complex today and teachers who have always struggled to provide a curriculum of relevant linguistic skills, knowledge and attitudes which keeps pace with children's needs are evermore hard-pressed to do so.

However many languages teachers may claim to 'know', with however extensive a knowledge of vocabulary in each, they need to develop conscious, analytical knowledge to use their language skills to the full benefit of children in the multilingual classroom. It is a romantic and unprofessional notion to expect bilingual teachers, simply by being bilingual, to meet all the needs of pupils whose home language they may share, just as it is unprofessional to expect that untrained adults who speaks only English can provide for the needs of pupils who only speak English. Of course a teacher who shares a bilingual child's home language has a huge beginning advantage over one who does not, but this advantage may be largely unexploited by the bilingual who does not make appropriate use of explicit linguistic knowledge. On the other hand, bilingual skills may be arduously gained by the 'monolingual' teacher. The gap in initial advantage may be tempered by other professional and personal qualities, chief among them being informed cultural empathy and energetic belief in children's potential. One concern of this book is to dispel some of the simplistic and professionally divisive assumptions which are made about 'monolingualism' and 'bilingualism' and, additionally, to counter an attitude which views some languages as 'belonging' to certain kinds of people, e.g. so-called 'Asian' languages to people whose origins are in the sub-continent and so-called 'European' languages to white people.

There are as many variations in linguistic competence among teachers as there are teachers. As all bilinguals know, the development of each of their languages depends on the contexts in which it is used, and so it is natural that some aspects of each language, vocabulary in particular, will be stronger or weaker than in the other language(s). By presuming that 'bilinguals' can and 'monolinguals' cannot draw on children's bilingualism we waste the latent skills of 'monolingual' and 'bilingual' teachers alike. This book sets out to give teachers insights into English vocabulary as a prime means of supporting children's access to a curriculum which is not limited by the English language. By providing an outline of how English words 'behave' to communicate meanings, I hope to show how this knowledge may be used strategically by children to develop command of English, which they need for successful curriculum learning, and consciousness of word-meaning which will enhance their bilingual potential.

A frequently expressed anxiety of teachers is that many children, whether their first language is English or whether they use English as an additional language (EAL pupils) have 'limited vocabulary', or 'poor range' of language. This book aims to show that children's success in curriculum learning depends on active involvement in building a complex network of linguistic meaning. Children's vocabulary development is not just a matter of acquiring more colourful adjectives for story or poetry writing, or a collection of technical terms for science and mathematics, important as these are. It is much more to do with developing a mental lexicon that is powered by semantic curiosity and the confidence to share ideas about the world. The development of vocabulary is linked both to cognition and to cultural experience: words always mean more than we think.

The book provides teachers with an understanding of how words work to convey meaning and offers a collection of strategies for supporting children's cross-curricular learning at the same time as extending their vocabulary, primarily in English but also in other languages. The five chapters approach vocabulary development in different ways, all of them taking account of children who are learning English in addition to a different home/community language and children whose only home language is English:

I.   The words we use, whether in English or in other languages, may be seen to behave in patterned ways as agents of meaning-making in linguistic and cultural systems. Teachers, whether or not we share pupils' home languages, are first and foremost model meaning-seekers, not only in relation to the school curriculum, but in far-reaching aspects of children's learning about the world. Whether we cater for children's learning across the whole curriculum or teach in particular subject areas, we need a *teacher consciousness* of patterns of 'lexical behaviour' – that is, ways of recognising how words work to convey meanings. Chapter One draws on common but largely unconscious knowledge about language (KAL) to outline a framework of knowledge about lexical behaviours. This framework is expanded in later chapters for its potential as a set of developmental indicators, as a guide for planning vocabulary development, and, most importantly, as a means of establishing an active classroom ethos of shared enthusiasm for exploring word-meaning in English and across language boundaries.

II. A key factor in pupils' achievement is their teacher's understanding of how learners learn words. Young children's development of lexicon (vocabulary) in a second language appears, in broad terms, to follow the same patterns that we can discern in first language acquisition (L_1). Older children who are at early stages of learning English as an additional language (EAL learners) can also be seen to operate in patterns similar to younger L_1 learners, but with important differences in lexical development and communicative strategies. Chapter Two picks out features of first language lexical development in order to provide indicators of proficiency in EAL.

III. School provides a huge range of language learning opportunities for children – in both National Curriculum programmes of study and in broader intellectual and cultural dimensions. For many, including English mother-tongue children, the language of school differs greatly from the language of the home and community, and this may be particularly dramatic in their experiences of reading and writing. Abstract and figurative meanings occur frequently in classroom talk and EAL pupils must grapple with English vocabulary of ever-increasing complexity as they grow older. Some curriculum areas make specific demands on children's lexical knowledge of which we are well aware, for example in the technical vocabulary of science or mathematics, but all subject areas use words which may cause difficulties unnoticed by teachers. How do we reconcile the content demands of National Curriculum subjects with the lexical demands of an additional language? Do we need a lexical syllabus for EAL pupils as they progress through Key Stage programmes? How can Key Stage planning attend to word-meaning in ways which benefit rather than burden teachers and learners? Chapter Three looks at how attention to words and their meanings can improve EAL pupils' learning in different curriculum areas.

IV. However systematic an approach we might plan for teaching English vocabulary in multilingual classrooms, our success will depend on how pupils engage in the processes affectively as well as academically. Full command of English vocabulary is a prime linguistic target for all pupils, but it is not the only one, and for many children it is of itself an unlikely achievement without a school ethos which promotes the linguistic potential of all pupils and all teachers beyond monolingualism. The culture of the classroom is multi-dimensional and ever-changing, and each child affects and is affected by it in complex and life-long ways. Whether or not a teacher shares a pupil's home language, be it English or another language, each child comes to the classroom from a culture of home which is different from school culture, and in ever-increasing numbers of classrooms the range of children's and teachers' home languages makes it more likely that some children's home language will be different from their teacher's home language. English vocabulary then becomes not only essential for access to curriculum knowledge but also, and even more crucially, the means of shared cultural referencing upon which learners and teachers are dependent for belonging with each other in a common purpose. Languages do not belong to people, but people find belonging through language. Chapter Four explores how teachers and learners can negotiate word-meanings together, in English and other languages, in a climate of 'cultural belonging'.

V. In Chapter Five a number of activities and resources are examined – for the principles they embody and for the practical benefits they offer teachers and learners to explore word-meaning in English and other languages. Words have an enduring fascination for all humans, and the best thing about developing word-power is that it is invariably enjoyable, even when it feels like work! We have only to look at the popularity of word quiz games on TV, at the stacked boxes in toy shops, at puzzle books by the supermarket checkout, to realise that word-meaning exploration is enjoyed hugely out-side the classroom. Activities that bring imagination, humour and intrigue into the classroom will always be needed and, when they go hand in hand with nurturing success in curriculum subjects, should not be viewed as treats or time-fillers. They deserve pride of place in a 'word-aware' curriculum for all children.

> *– What do you call a one-eyed dinosaur?*
>
> *– A Doyouthinkitsawus.*

Chapter One

Words for teachers

All UK classrooms are actually or potentially multilingual and children with language skills who can build bridges between different cultural groups are blessed. The two main guiding principles of this book are that all UK children need a full command of standard English in their linguistic repertoire, and that every child also needs an understanding of the role of language in intercultural communication – ideally by developing bilingual skills beyond simple transactional use to a level of bicultural participation. The National Curriculum General Requirements for English: Key Stages 1-4 (1995) provide a rubric for these ideas:

> In order for children to participate confidently in public, cultural and working life, pupils need to be able to speak, write and read standard English fluently and accurately. All pupils are therefore entitled to the full range of opportunities necessary to enable them to develop competence in standard English. The richness of dialects and other languages can make an important contribution to pupils' knowledge and understanding of standard English. Where appropriate, pupils should be encouraged to make use of their understanding and skills in other languages when learning English. (DfE, 1995)

For all that this is a legal requirement whose underlying tone appears to make linguistic knowledge the servant of 'competence in standard English', the statement provides teachers with opportunities to work in a far more satisfying scenario – children developing competence and creativity in language repertoires which *include* standard English.

Many UK children who use English[1] for 'school language' and one or more different languages (often including varieties of English) for 'home language' achieve well in the UK school system, though I hope to show how, through attention to word-meaning in the vocabularies of English and their home languages, their achievement may be further enhanced. A common factor in the under-achievement of many other children for whom English is an additional language, and also for a significant number of children whose first language is

English, is poor development of English lexicon. It has become something of a truism to say that all teachers are language teachers and it is generally understood that, at nursery, reception and at every stage thereafter, all areas of the curriculum make linguistic demands on children that teachers need to take account of. Among these demands, the development of vocabulary (or *lexicon*, a term I shall use interchangeably with *vocabulary*) is recognised as vitally important by all teachers. Children are ill-equipped to handle the ideas content of the curriculum if they do not have command of the words and phrases (*lexical units*) that different topics or different subjects employ. However, the vocabulary with which children operate in the classroom is not confined to the collections of specialist terms that curriculum subjects generate. When we look at the glossaries of well-designed topic books we quickly find that 'key words' are relatively easily identifiable and we are not unhappy about this because we expect to have to pay attention to these and to have to teach their meanings quite explicitly. What is not so obvious is that many more words and phrases are used in the total pattern of classroom discourse in ways which affect children's access to the ideas they are learning about.

If you are a teacher in a UK classroom then you are an adept adult user of English, whether you regard English as your only language or as just one language in a wider personal linguistic repertoire. You use English in fluent, rapid patterns and, whilst there are many occasions when you attend carefully to the words you use with children, there are many more times when the pace of classroom interaction makes it impossible to attend to words *per se*. Children (of all ages) who are at early stages of acquiring English as an additional language (EAL pupils[2]) usually attend closely to their teacher's words with the instinctive aim of finding meaning in the words they discern as most significant in a sentence, or string of sentences. This strategy works well for young children in nursery and reception classrooms where a teacher's words are very often accompanied by actions or by use of real objects, pictures and the like, so that the meanings of verbal utterances are supported by non-verbal contextual clues. It is also one of the best strategies available to older EAL beginners, although more formal patterns of teacher-pupil interaction provide fewer non-verbal clues to lexical meaning. Older EAL beginners are generally able to draw on more sophisticated metalinguistic knowledge in order to home in on 'key words'. More about this later. What I want to do just now is set the scene for my focus on *lexical meaning*.

Knowledge About Language (KAL)[3]

Word meaning is an area of second language pedagogy that has been neglected in favour of others. A quick survey of 'methods' of second language teaching in recent years shows that attention has shifted from teaching grammatical structures in patterned exercises, to focusing on the 'functions and notions' of communication and, more recently, to 'immersion' and 'whole language' approaches. I am not going to compare these 'methods'. Each encompasses a wide school of thought and highly varied practical classroom application. Each has been expounded in an educational epoch which has influenced them and been influenced by them and this has cumulatively led to inter-disciplinary dialogue between linguists and educationalists. As yet though, teachers of EAL children in UK classrooms have not been able to avail themselves readily of the rich bank of ideas about word meaning that theoretical linguistics provides.

Theoretical linguistics gives us a number of vantage points to examine the role of word meaning in classrooms where young children are developing their command of English as an additional language (EAL) and at the same time are using English as their main means of access to the primary curriculum. Under the general influence of 'holistic' approaches to L_1 language development, current frameworks for teaching young EAL learners in the UK make little direct application of linguistic theory. In practice, 'frameworks' for teaching

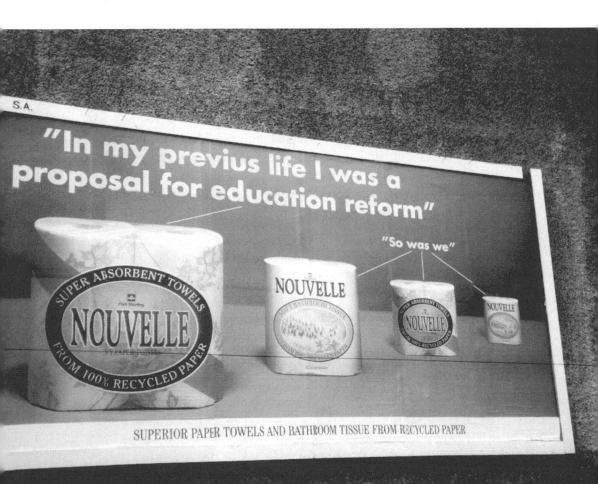

EAL pupils reside mainly in local education authorities' or schools' language policies and though these may be founded on sound educational principles they rarely apply theoretical linguistic paradigms. As a result, opportunities for EAL learners to benefit from a rich body of knowledge about language have been overlooked.

Attention to the needs of EAL pupils in UK National Curriculum documents is scant, although this glaring inadequacy in DfEE documents has in some measure been redressed by the School Curriculum and Assessment Authority (1996). The UK National Curriculum (DfE, 1995) includes explicit requirements for attention to words, and of course this forms part of the statutory entitlement for all pupils. In English Key Stage One, the 'Standard English and Language Study' includes requirements that:

> Pupils' vocabulary should be extended through activities that encourage their interest in words, including exploration and discussion of:
> - the meanings of words and their use and interpretation in different contexts
> - words with similar and opposite meanings
> - word games
> - words associated with specific occasions, e.g. greetings, celebrations; (DfE, 1995:4).
> - Pupils' interest in words and their meanings should be developed, and their vocabulary should be extended through consideration and discussion of words with similar meanings, opposites, and words with more than one meaning (DfE, 1995: 10).
> - discussion of more imaginative and adventurous choices of words
> - consideration of groups of words, e.g. word families, the range of words relevant to a topic (DfE, 1995: 12).
> - Pupils should be taught to distinguish between words of similar meaning, to explain the meanings of words and to experiment with choices of vocabulary (DfE, 1995: 16).
>
> [These extracts from Standard English and Language Study in the English Orders are incomplete.]

Regrettably, much of the detailed 'knowledge about language' (KAL) first expounded by the Kingman and the Cox Reports (DES, 1988 and 1989) and subsequently by the professional development materials for teachers from the LINC programme (HMSO, 1990) has been ignored by, if not expunged from National Curriculum documents as they currently stand (see Cox, 1995). As a consequence, attention to the lexical (and other) needs of EAL pupils is virtually absent from Statutory Orders. Separation of 'English' from other curriculum areas in the documented presentation of the Orders does not of itself imply separation in theoretical, philosophical or practical terms. However, as far as lexical meaning is concerned, in the National Curriculum Orders (1995) for the eight other subject areas references are limited to mention of 'technical' vocabulary of each subject. This leaves serious gaps in attention to the role of language in different curriculum areas, and leaves teachers, who may or may not have had training in the needs of EAL pupils, to make their own links between the development of English and the content of each subject area.

The whole business of language development – both L_1 and L_2 is so complex that we have to chop it up if we're going to get anywhere with any of it in ways which make a difference to the educational achievement of pupils. And that of course is our goal. While teachers' KAL and its general application in the primary classroom is considerable, much of this knowledge is implicit rather than explicit: analytical knowledge of lexical meaning is not generally part of teacher consciousness. Bilingual teachers who share the first language of their pupils have some advantages over monolingual colleagues in alertness to some of the comprehension difficulties that English vocabulary causes EAL pupils, but their knowledge about word-meaning cannot be assumed to be explicit and analytical any more than monolingual teacher knowledge. An on-going study (McWilliam, in progress) indicates wide variation in teacher consciousness of the role of word-meaning in L_2 development.

This chapter looks at a body of knowledge about words that teachers can draw on in order to understand some of the linguistic processing that all pupils are involved in at the same time as learning subject ideas; it looks at what 'vocabulary' amounts to, and at the ways that words 'behave' to convey meaning. The main aim of this chapter is to establish a framework of 'lexical behaviours' which teachers can use to support the learning of all their pupils but more especially of pupils whose developing command of English as the medium of curriculum learning is an addition to home/community language repertoire.

KAL is something we all have, not because we are teachers, but because we are human. Our store of linguistic 'nouse' has been growing since babyhood and whether we speak one, two or several languages, we all share a human pool of KAL which serves us pretty well for our everyday communicative needs. This store of 'metalinguistic' knowledge is largely unconscious – but we do attend consciously to our knowledge about language on many occasions – perhaps when we have to speak publicly, when we play a word game, when we compose a formal letter. In other words, when we pay attention to words.

The complex and prolonged learning process that we went through in acquiring our first language is very largely forgotten, although I am willing to bet that you can recall some cameos of childhood miscomprehension. However, the learning processes that you may have gone through or may now be going through in an *additional* language could provide more conscious and memorable data to draw on. Past and on-going personal language experience is your greatest source of KAL, but until it becomes conscious, explicit and informed knowledge it remains largely unexploited. Teachers' KAL is of course professionally informed, both by theoretical study of child language and cognitive development and by empirical experience of children's comprehension and performance in the classroom context. I hope to show that enough of your existing personal KAL and teacher KAL can rapidly and enjoyably be made explicit and so affect your consciousness of how vocabulary behaves in your classroom.

Grammar and intonation

Our knowledge about language (KAL) is much greater than our knowledge of vocabulary. We know that words and phrases have to fit into a language system in order to 'make sense'. Words have to follow each other in sequence as they are spoken or as they take shape on paper or on the computer screen and this

sequence must obey conventions of grammar which vary from one language to another. If words are the building bricks of our speech or writing, grammar is the cement that holds the building together.

In all language systems, words are put together in conventional (and sometimes unconventional) groups to form the syntactic (grammatical) units that we usually call sentences. Words occurring in sentences therefore represent meanings through their relations with each other, and this grammatical relationship is one of the major determinants of the meanings of the words. So although our focus is with word-meaning (lexical semantics), I will often refer to the grammatical use of words. In spite of the inseparability of words from grammar, we can put grammar aside and explore words and word meaning in ways which add to the current state of understanding development in L_1 and L_2.

Spoken words are produced in sound sequences which follow patterns of intonation characteristic of the particular language, and often of the dialect of the speaker. Our understanding of a speaker's words is drawn not solely from the meanings we attribute to the words themselves, but from varying patterns of intonation. Intonation is used in English to vary the stress on words, the pitch and tune of a sentence, and can thereby convey a collection of different meanings without any change in word sequence. Other languages employ intonation differently, and this dimension of 'meaning-making' causes difficulties for EAL learners up to very advanced stages. It is of course an aspect of linguistic proficiency that matures slowly in L_1, and English mother-tongue (EL_1) children often fail to discern the different meanings intended by this variation of stress.

Try out these examples with EL_1 children and EAL children of different ages and stages, giving stress to different words in turn:

So you're doing the washing-up.

Give me the book.

I'm not going there again.

So when we look at word-meaning, we have to maintain an awareness that spoken words are used in patterns of discourse where speakers have intentions of meaning which may not trigger change in their choice of words, but may be put into effect by voiced intonation.

Attention to Words

Vocabulary is a word teachers use comfortably. We all know what it means: the words and phrases that make up a language. We know that vocabulary is something different from grammar and different from pronunciation or spelling. (We know that we need these too.) We know that the vocabulary of a language can be classified as nouns, verbs, adjectives, adverbs and other word 'types' (though we may be vaguer about the others!). We know, and in fact we have known since early childhood, that vocabulary is what we need first and foremost for communicating ideas.

We put great value on vocabulary, admiring a speaker or writer who uses a 'rich range' and judging a 'limited range' as a deficiency. This value is not usually based on linguistic analysis: it is generally based on one view of the speaker's ability to 'get their message across', or of the writer's effect on our feelings. Our subjective judgements about a person's vocabulary (including our own) are generalised and impressionistic in most everyday encounters. Are they any more systematic or analytical in the classroom?

Words are unconsciously viewed by most people as generally *denotative*, that is, as possessing 'informative power' which we can be quite clear about. But this is a view we modify on occasions when we recognise the 'affective power' (terms used by Graddol, Cheshire and Swann, 1987) of words we use for such different jobs as persuading others to our point of view, justifying our actions, speculating about the future, etc.

When we come across words we don't know or are unsure of, we consult dictionaries and thesauri in expectation of authoritative definitions and rules of 'correct usage'. Dictionaries are written by other human beings whose ideas have been shaped by linguistic fashions over the years, but children and many adults are unaware of this. We expect dictionaries to give us information about words that we can rely.

We all know, even if we don't try it, that if we want to learn a new language we have to learn its vocabulary. We each have a subjective sense of our own 'command' of vocabulary in the language or languages we know, and we generally assess our own proficiency in a language by how much of its vocabulary we know.

We are also wary of words, and quite often need to check that they are working for and not agin us. 'What do you mean, exactly?', we find ourselves saying in conversation, or 'That's not quite what I meant' ..... On occasions we have a well-developed sensitivity about how our words are being interpreted by our audience; at other times we can be amazed at how our words are erroneously reported. We all know that words can be dangerous weapons.

So we have a plenty of ideas about words but we are rather taking for granted that we know what a word is, that we can define the word *word*. Words are the bunches of letters that we use all the time in the classroom, pointing to them, writing them, underlining them. So let us say for now that a word is a collection of letters with, when it is written, a space on either side. This is easy to see when a string of words is written down using the normal spacing conventions of the roman alphabet. It does not work as a definition when words are spoken. Spoken words are produced as continual strings (in short or long utterances) of sound. One of the first jobs a learner of a new language has to do when trying to make sense of a spoken utterance is to discern some of the word boundaries – i.e. where one word ends and another begins.

See what sense you get out of the text below – first try reading it to yourself, and then try reading it aloud...

Un petit d'un petit
S'étonne aux Halles
Un petit d'un petit
Ah! degrés te fallent
Indolent qui ne sort cesse
Indolent qui ne se mène
Qu'importe un petit d'un petit
Tout Gai de Reguennes.

source: Luis d'Antin Van Rooten, *Mots d'Heures: Gousses, Rames, The d'Atin Manuscript* (1977 edition)

You've probably got it by now, but if you're still struggling, turn to p.186 to understand what it is all about.

Now of course you 'understand' the whole 'text', don't you? The difficulties you had are akin to the difficulties experienced by early stage EAL pupils who hear a long string of English sentences and are unable to pick out enough words to glean meaning for the whole 'text'. If you know some French you were probably able to make something out of some small bits of the text, but even if you are a native French speaker you will have been puzzled by much of it. If it fell into place for you before you turned to p.186 for the answer, think – what made the penny drop? Not any of the individual words or the meanings you tried to attach to them. Not your attempts at translation into English or another language. If you had no idea at all what it was all about when you turned to p.186, you didn't do any worse than others I know who meet this for the first time.

So now try this one – you'll be able to make sense of this much faster, because you know what the game is now. Read aloud as you did before...

Chacun Gille
Houer ne taupe de hile
Tôt-fait, j'appelle au boiteur
Chaque fêle dans un broc, est-ce crosne?
Un Gille qu'aime tant berline à fêtard.

source: Luis d'Antin Van Rooten, *Mots d'Heures: Gousses, Rames, The d'Atin Manuscript* (1977 edition)

Got it? Of course, but check your answer on p.186.

But I bet you are still finding it difficult to read the text aloud. Your difficulties are compounded by confused expectations of word boundaries and by unfamiliar phoneme/grapheme correspondence – even though you 'know' what it says. Perhaps you are also trying to apply your KAL (of French?) in trying to make grammatical meaning out of the words in the way they hang together. People who handle more than one language may have advantages here, but inhibitions (or fixed expectations) can interfere in discerning the word boundaries that match with our expectations of word/meaning matches.

Once you understand how this works, each piece eventually falls into place as a whole 'text'. You make sense of it by a near-enough match with prior cultural knowledge of nursery rhymes. And then, at this stage, you *stop attending to the detail of the words*. Once you've got the whole message, you don't need to worry about the constituent parts anymore. You don't want to spend any more time on the *form*, you have what you need out of the overall message.

This is exactly what many EAL pupils experience when they are confronted by 'texts', spoken or written, whose density of form – of unfamiliar words and phrases – is too demanding. If they manage to make sense of the overall message, they do not spend time or energy on attending to its *constituent parts*, particularly if a well-intentioned teacher is on hand to 'simplify' or to provide the 'answer'. When they meet the same words and phrases elsewhere and struggle again to make meaning from them, it may well be that they will be 'helped' in a way that again takes their attention away from the words – the building blocks of the message – and so a damaging habit may quickly be acquired.

Eve Clark (1993) makes the point that it is no easy matter for young children learning their first language to isolate word forms: success depends on children's close attention to the adult's use of language. This attention to words is a crucial element in successful teaching and learning in multilingual classrooms.

Attention to theory of lexical meaning

Attention to words, the lexical form of human communication, has been going on for as long as we have written history and no doubt before. The Russian psychologist Lev Vygotsky, writing in 1934, has given us the much-quoted statement from the more philosophical end of a wide spectrum of linguistic theory: 'A word is a microcosm of human consciousness.'

Other attempts to explain what word meaning is all about lie in the fields of lexical semantics and first order logic. D.A. Cruse (1986) writes:

... we can picture the meaning of a word as a pattern of affinities and disaffinities with all the other words in the language with which it is capable of contrasting semantic relations in grammatical contexts.

Cruse (1986:3) makes the distinction between 'closed set items' and 'open set items' in order to characterise the grammatical and the lexical elements of sentences. With respect, I adapt his example to suit the cultural context in which teachers might use it with EAL pupils:

Typically, closed set items have few or no possibilities of substitution in an actual sentence:

Shakil's kindness amazed   Shameem.
                   amazes

They comprise affixes (*dis*like, kind*ness*, Shakil'*s*, wait*ed*, com*ing*, black*en*, etc.) and independent words (sometimes called markers) such as articles, conjunctions, prepositions, a major part of whose linguistic function is to signal the grammatical organisation of sentences. The open set elements, on the other hand, are those which belong to classes which are subject to a relatively rapid turnover in membership as new terms are coined and others fall into obsolescence. They are the lexical roots – the principal meaning-bearing elements in a sentence. (The open set elements [above] are *Shakil, kind, amaze,* and *Shameem.*) They typically have numerous possibilities of substitution in a sentence:

Shakil's	kindness	amazed	Shameem
Amrik-	cool-	amuse-	Sue
Rifat-	rude-	disturb-	John
Yasmeen-	sad-	shock-	Baljit
etc.	etc.	etc.	etc.

adapted from Cruse (1986:3)

Cruse adds a pertinent note about the way this distinction may vary in different languages:

It should be noted that semantic notions which are expressed in one language grammatically (i.e. by means of closed set items) may well be expressed in another language lexically (i.e. by means of open set items). (Cruse, 1986:20)

I ask you to allow that the term 'word' stands for the individual unit bounded by spaces (when written) such as *egg, telephone, Tyrannosaurus*; for compound words which work as units, e.g. *egghead; telephone kiosk; Tyrannosaurus Rex,* and also for phrases or 'word-chunks' that work as meaning units such that their sense is lost if the words are separated, for example *don't count your chickens before they're hatched; on the grape-vine.; as dead as a dodo*. More properly I should use the term 'lexical unit' or 'lexeme'.

Lexical units

table	telephone	Tyrannosaurus
table-tennis	telephone kiosk	Tyrannosaurus Rex
pizza	spaghetti	tiramisu
bon appetit	hors d'œuvres	
set the table	hear it on the grapevine	
dead as a dodo	without so much as a by-your-leave	

Richards *et al* (1992) provide a user-friendly definition of *lexeme* and *lexical unit:*

> the smallest unit in the meaning system of a language that can be distinguished from other similar units. A lexeme [lexical unit] is an abstract unit. It can occur in many different forms in actual spoken or written sentences, and is regarded as the same lexeme even when inflected.

> For example, in English, all inflected forms such as *give, gives, given, giving, gave* would belong to the one lexeme *give.*

> Similarly, such expressions as *bury the hatchet, hammer and tongs, give up,* and *white paper* would each be considered a single lexeme. (1992:210)

Content words and imaging

In a similar way, words are broadly divided by Jean Aitchison (1987) into two types – **function words** and **content words**. Take this utterance, for example, to see the two types:

> It was *midnight* when we *collapsed wearily* into *bed* after *trudging home* through the *howling blizzard.*

It is the **content** words, the words which are generally meant when we talk about lexicon, the mental store and management/operation of words, that we are concerned with here.

The distinctions of word types provided by Cruse and those provided by Aitchison together do a good job of identifying the words and phrases which EAL learners need to attend to in building their lexicon. We need *function* words (or *closed set* items) to operate properly (whether in a 'standard' dialect of English, other varieties of English or any other language) and I do not in any way wish to belittle the need for EAL pupils to develop grammatical competences. I am, however, arguing that *content* words (as they form lexical units) merit particular kinds of attention by teachers and pupils in multilingual classrooms.

One of my main reasons for proposing focused attention on *content* words (to use Aitchison's term) is because of their very obvious semantic difference from *function* words: they are the words to which we can attach **images**. You will easily pick out the most 'imageful' words and phrases in the following newspaper extract:

> A *frail kitten* which was *dumped* and *left for dead* in a *slaughterhouse* has made a *miraculous recovery.*
>
> The *female cat* was *discovered clinging* to the *dead bodies* of her *mother*, *brother* and two *sisters* in the building on W---- Lane, Bradford.
>
> She has been *nursed back to health* by ---- at the *Cat Rescue Centre* in ----.
>
> 'Her *eyes* were *badly ulcerated* and were *sore,*' said Mrs ---- 'We were *horrified* when we saw her.'
>
> Mrs ---- is looking to find an *owner* to offer the *cat* a *caring home.*
>
> The Centre is also *appealing* for help in *raising funds* to keep it going.
>
> *Bradford Star* (free community newspaper) no. 831 March 1997.

It is the content words in this text that provide readers with the collection of **images** we need if we are to enter into the scenario being reported. The function words are also necessary for each sentence to make grammatical sense, and for the text to be understandable as a coherent narrative. But the images evoked by the content words are what motivate us to read, or, if the story had been read to us, to listen.

The images evoked here are not simply visual, although our mental processing of the text involves assembling a set of cultural 'pictures' from our stored knowledge (accurate or otherwise) of kittens, slaughterhouses, ulcers, Cat Rescue Centres etc. I use the word 'image' in the sense proposed by Earl Stevick (1986), who developed a language teaching approach based on use of mental imagery and on memory networks that draw on learners' cultural knowledge:

> An image is something that we perceive (more or less vividly, and in many more ways that merely visual) as a result of the interaction between what we have in storage and what is going on at the moment (1986: 11).

Imaging is a way of drawing on multi-sensory associations – of sight, sound, touch, taste, smell, as well as the many other physical sensations (e.g. feeling sick, feeling energetic) and human emotions (sympathy, hesitation, amusement etc.). We collect these multi-sensory associations to build images and make 'human sense' out of the words we hear or read. Equally, when we are speaking and writing to communicate to an audience our own stored images, we try to match our choice of content words as best we can with those collected multi-sensory associations.

Stevick (1976) reminds us that: 'the very utterances of words, regardless of how well or how poorly they are pronounced, depend on sources far beyond the linguistic level (1976: 64)'. He is emphasising the mental processing – 'imaging' – that language-learners must undertake in matching L_2 lexicon with their prior knowledge of the world. In Stevick's view, neglect of this dimension of language-learning by teachers can quickly lead to student demotivation. If teachers are overly concerned about accuracy in pronunciation and grammar, particularly at early stages of additional language learning, the real reasons for using words – i.e. communicating images, is lost.

Stevick (1986) advocates '**shared imaging**' as a means of enhancing students' memory of new vocabulary in the language they are learning. He encourages FL learners to talk about their mental images in the classroom with teacher and peers because doing so enables students to make memorable connections between new words and 'imageful' cultural experience. I discuss this particular use of classroom talk with EAL children in Chapter 4. The point I want to make now is that for EAL learners (and for English mother-tongue learners too) the development of lexicon is only part of the vastly more complex mental processing that each human being is involved in – making sense of the world and their own role in it. Imaging, as a classroom strategy, is founded on the human instinct to communicate through words what is in our heads and our hearts, and to test our own match of words and perceptions against those of other people.

Matching words with meaning

We acquire word meanings in the process of attaching images to them. New words that are encountered by all children and adults in cognitively demanding situations have, in varying duration, the status of 'suspended meaning'. The words lack image or puzzle us because our images for them are vague or confused. Such words may have 'pending' entries in our lexicon, our personal mental dictionary, so that we are unlikely to operate them confidently.

The meanings represented by some words are fairly easily worked out by EAL (and L_1) learners, and are fairly easy to teach – words which label objects, animals and people, i.e. realia or 'concrete referents' that we can point to, touch or hold. However, we cannot assume that because the job of labelling concrete referents is fairly easy, the learners will automatically know them. We do know that for young learners (in L_1 and L_2) an experiential approach to learning to 'label' things with words is best, so that the words can be stored as representations of the multi-sensory encounters with the objects.

The real world objects represented by the words below for example, may be easily collected and manipulated by young children. Some of the words that label them in English will be new to English mother-tongue children too. Matching words to the objects may seem to be a fairly straightforward process, although the new words need to be modelled and repeated may times over for EAL learners. There is after all a one to one correspondence between each English word and its real world refcrent. But is there? We only have to look at some of the words in relation to each other to begin to see that labelling involves making judgements based on multi-sensory perceptions. Take for example the words *stone* and *pebble*; *nail* and *screw*; or *cup* and *tumbler*. In order to attach these words to their real world referents – stones and pebbles, nails and screws, cups and tumblers, children need to attend to the properties of each object by touching as well as looking.

cardboard box	twig	chalk	paper clip
teddy	nail	foil	rubber
stone	plastic pen	marble	glass tumbler
foam	wool	candle	wooden ruler
plasticine	straw	shell	ping pong ball
cork	brass screw	plastic cup	pebble

(An activity developed by G. Hardy and and M. Dunne)

Meaning-making involves *differentiating* words from each other. Until our imaging provides us with the differentiation we cannot operate the words effectively. This means that learning the meaning of each word must involve us in referring to the other words and their images. So when does a twig become a branch? a nail become a screw? a stone become a pebble? Theoretical linguistics is much occupied by such instances when the 'correct' lexical label may be a matter of dispute.

There seems to be a common human propensity to spend time on such problems. It may be interesting to see the range of disagreement among a group of colleagues about labelling the concrete objects in the picture above. If you are a multilingual group your variable range of labels will call into question issues of translating 'equivalent' words. You will find yourselves questioning one another's ideas about the properties the objects *need* in order to qualify for one

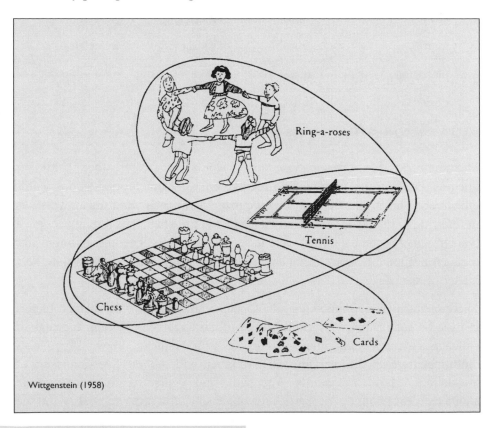

Labov (1973)

label rather than another; you will begin to judge that some properties are more *central* than others, and you will hear each other talking about *typical* instances of the objects – very often in relation to their function in cultural contexts. These ideas of 'necessity, centrality and typicality' are discussed in some detail by Ray Jackendoff (1983) who examines how such lexical judgements affect and are affected by perception and cognition.

Ring-a-roses

Tennis

Chess

Cards

Wittgenstein (1958)

Even more difficult to agree on are words which label *abstract* ideas. What, for example, makes a game a game? What properties constitute the 'necessity, centrality and typicality' of 'gamehood'? Try asking your colleagues!

If words for labelling objects and activities which we take for granted are so complex, what of some other easy words that we expect L_2 learners to use as labels? In our collection of labels for real world objects we have some lexical items formed by word compounds – *paper clip, cardboard box* and *ping pong ball*. Such lexical items are first acquired as 'chunks' and young EAL learners who hear rather than read them will not discern the internal boundaries of the compound. English uses a great many compounds in this way and so the words *ball, box* and *clip* occur in combination with many other words, forming such compounds as:

ballpoint pen	clipboard	chocolate box
ball-boy/ball-girl	hair clip	phone box
tennis ball	film clip	signal box
rugby ball	bulldog clip	lunch box
ball-cock		box office
		box number

Many such words come into use when a new commodity or development of technology prompts 'coinage' of compounds. It is easy for fluent adult speakers to see that compound words like these are built around the 'root' meaning of a word but it is far from obvious to young EAL learners.

Polysemy (multiple meanings)

Compound words are one form of **collocation**, the way words keep company with each other to make meanings. So far I have used compound words as examples of collocation which are used to label real world objects, but words collocate in many more ways than this. Words keep each other company in short phrases and their potential for meaning is therefore vastly greater. Note how *ball, box* and *clip* can be used to form the chunks of meaning we use as **idioms**:

– the ball's in your court

– a clip round the earhole

– did you watch the box last night?

The 'root' words have acquired quite different meanings from their former function as labels. English uses many hundreds (probably thousands) of idiomatic expressions like these – as do other languages. They are largely used as unanalysed chunks or formulas by fluent speakers and they make up a substantial proportion of everyday speech.

Words often collocate in clusters to give coherence to a text, as in the two examples below.

FRUITFUL™
FROM
Shredded Wheat™

Full of fruit - Full of taste

Enjoy succulent *sultanas* combined with plump *raisins* dried in the California sun and blended with *hazelnut* pieces. Crunchy slices of golden *banana*, mixed with juicy pieces of *papaya* and tender toasted *coconut*.

Discover the tempting taste that's bursting with delicious fruits and crunchy whole wheat goodness.

Goodness never tasted so good!

Great Adventures Catamaran and pontoon on the Outer Barrier Reef

Gateway to the spectacular Great Barrier Reef Marine Park, blessed with a wonderful tropical climate and a wealth of additional attractions, Cairns is one of Australia's most popular holiday destinations. Inland, lie sugarcane plantations, waterfalls and lush rainforests whilst to the north are the secluded beach resorts of Palm Cove and Port Douglas and even further north, the spectacular Daintree Rainforest and historic Cooktown.

Very few words in a language maintain a consistency of meaning when they collocate with other words. The English words *box, chalk, clip, nail, foil, stone, foam, shell, cork, screw, cup* which I used earlier as **nouns** to label real world objects may also be used grammatically as **verbs** to express actions, and they can also function grammatically as a**djectives**, as single or compound words. What this tells us is that words are **polysemous** – they have multiple meanings which change according to the context in which they occur, and they have grammatical functions which differ in different utterances. The polysemous nature of words like these is obvious to us as fluent adult speakers of English because we have had years of experience in hearing, speaking, reading and writing them. Younger or newer learners of English have to work all this out and, until they do so, their comprehension and productive use of the words is severely limited.

> TAKE
>
> take a class
>
> take a sandwich
>
> take a photo
>
> take a break..

The multiple meanings of some words raises arguments among linguists (see Lyons, 1995) about the distinction between words which are polysemous and words which are **homonyms.** There are two kinds of homonyms: different words that coincidentally sound the same as each other, such as *pain* and *pane*, or *feet* and *feat* (these are **homophones**), and words which appear the same when written but have different pronunciations, for example, *bow* and *bow*; or *tear* and *tear* (these are **homographs**).

Without entering into the linguistic debate, we can see the problem with some of the word-meanings already explored: *box* a container and *box* the act of fighting; *clip* in *paper-clip* and *hair-clip*, and *clip* in *film-clip* and *hedge-clipping*. Are these the same words used with different meanings or quite different words which just happen to sound the same? Some of these arguments can be settled by referring to an etymological dictionary (although these too are written by human beings!), others fuel debate in theoretical semantics. Lyons (1995) shows that *partial* homonymy can be caused by grammatical form:

The verbs 'find' and 'found' share the form *found*

Last (last week) and last (bricks last a long time)

rung (of a ladder) and *rung* (the bell was rung at midnight)

(Lyons, 1995: 55-58)

So, as well as acquiring meaning in the sorts of collocation mentioned so far i.e. in compound words or idiomatic phrases, words have additional meaning potential by virtue of their *form* which may belong to more than one grammatical class – e.g. as a noun, verb, adjective or adverb.

Partial homonyms are quite different from near homophones – words which sound nearly the same and may be confused by young learners (and in many instances by adults) who mishear or fail to note the difference in meaning between two words which sound similar. We all know examples of children's capacity for attaching their own meanings to words they 'mishear':

- the Aztec king who wanted more taxis

- apple saws

- electric currants

These were not spelling mistakes! The teachers who noted these examples of EAL children's misunderstanding encouraged the children to describe aloud the mental images they were constructing. The danger of accepting children's surface L_2 fluency as evidence of conceptual understanding became clear[4].

Near homophones may blur word boundaries or pick out phonemes to provide endless scope for children's jokes:

> Knock knock
>
> Who's there?
>
> Juno
>
> Juno who?
>
> Of course I do!

> What does a frog with bad eyesight do?
>
> Hop to the hoptician.

And we don't grow out of the habit of using them for varying effects:

> MORE REASONS TO SHOP AT MORRISONS

> NOW IS THE SEASON OF OUR DISCOUNT TENTS

> 'your chicken tikka makes my cheese sandwich look quite paltry'

Quite young children are sometimes aware of the problematics of homophones and polysemy. 'I had sponge pudding for school dinner' one eight-year old reported to his mum, 'but it wasn't the sort you have in the bath,' he added, just to make sure she didn't get the wrong idea. Some homophones are more puzzling: 'How can somebody die from a blow to the head?' another mum was asked. On other occasions it is difficult to work out whether words which cause confusion are polysemous lexical items or homonyms – *conductor*, *bulb* and *shoot* are some that have been reported from science activities[5].

> LET'S CZECH INTO WEMBLEY
> (1996 World Cup T-shirt slogan)

> COUGHING NAILS – cigarettes

> CUEDOS – name of a snooker hall

> You can bury that beret back in Bury

Let us now look at another selection of lexical units that look easy – they are phonemically regular, occur with high frequency and are likely to be met at early stages of EAL acquisition:

SET	LINE	BOOT	STAND
TOP	BOX	KID	TIP
BEAT	SAIL	HOT	HAND

Remember our idea of *imaging* as a way of attaching a mental representation of meaning to words. To do this for each of the words above we need to contextualise it – verbally in a phrase or sentence, and with a mental image. Take for example the word *set*. It has no meaning for us until we relate it to other words, which may be provided in the context in which we hear it or read it.

The *Longman Contemporary Dictionary of English* illustrates word-meanings as they are used in normal patterns of speech and writing. The listing on page 24 for *set* (much abbreviated!) is based on the variety of contexts in which the word occurs and gives an idea of how much we take the meanings of 'easy' words for granted.

Figurative meaning and literal meaning

This [incompletely quoted] range of meanings further illustrates one of the most important aspects of lexical semantics – the way many of the words we use are polysemous, and may be used for **figurative meaning** as well as for **literal meaning**. Take some of the other 'easy' words and note how they may be used in both ways:

SAIL	HAND
We're planning to sail on the six o'clock ferry	hold my hand
He sailed casually into the room	give me a hand
She sailed through her exams	you've got to hand it to him
You're sailing close to the wind	all hands on deck

Try out some of the others from page 24 with a colleague.

Many of these high-frequency lexical units (words and phrases) are used idiomatically with both literal and figurative meanings. So EAL pupils can flounder (sic) when understanding depends on discerning the intended meaning in relation to the context in which it occurs. Figurative expressions 'trip off our tongues' in everyday speech and are also used, perhaps more consciously, in prepared speech (as for example in TV news texts) and in writing. They are culturally generated – and many are so clichéd that we hardly think of them as metaphoric. On the other hand, when we are aware of this we might think that

SET (verb)

1. PUT DOWN

2. START SOMETHING HAPPENING   3. DECIDE, ESTABLISH

4. A TASK, SOMETHING TO DO   5. MAKE READY

6. MUSIC/BOOKS/FILMS   7. WANT/NOT WANT

8. OTHER MEANINGS: set a record;
an example; somebody straight; right; free/
loose; glue/cement; hair; set about; set against;
set apart; set aside; set forth; set off;
set up home; set up camp; [and many
more...]

SET (noun)

1. GROUP OF THINGS

2. TELEVISION/RADIO   3. STAGE

4. FILM   5. SPORT

6. MUSIC   7. HAIR

8. PEOPLE   9. FIRMNESS

10. PART OF BODY   11. STUDENTS

12. MATHS   13. ONION

SET (adjective)

1. PLACED

2. WAGE/TIME   3. a set book

4. a set menu   5. be set on/dead set on

6. have your heart set on   7. READY

8. a set smile   9. set opinions/beliefs

10. set in your ways   11. set to/likely to happen

Source: Longman Contemporary Dictionary of English

these figurative meanings are too difficult for EAL learners and try to exclude them from classroom talk. But if the teacher is the main model for EAL how are children going to meet them and have opportunities to explore them in ways which unravel their multiple meaning potential?

Similes are some of the more explicit metaphors that we use frequently:

as keen as mustard	as light as a feather
quick as a flash	like peas in a pod
like talking to a brick wall	like floating on air

you will be able to complete the rest, and perhaps find equivalents (equivalent *meanings*, not literal translations) in other languages:

as dry as...	as fit as...
as bright as...	as dull as...
as gentle as...	as fresh as...
as bold as...	like a lamb...
like a cat with...	caught like a rat...
swearing like...	like a ray of...
like a dose of...	like a bull in...

Lakoff and Johnson (1983) provide a wealth of evidence to show that figurative/ metaphoric meanings are impossible to exclude from natural speech, even if we want to. A colleague who was trying to avoid heavily loaded figurative speech with her EAL pupils was recording the pattern of talk in her classroom (Year 4) and said, 'Nazia, just go and see if that tape's still running'. Nazia went to check and came back to her to say, 'No it's not running, Miss. It's just going round and round.'[6] Another EAL pupil (Year 5) was asked the meaning of 'the foot of the mountain'. He could only guess it had something to do with socks...

Many of the metaphors we use are so common they may be referred to as 'dead', since the freshness of perception they once had is dulled by familiarity. But they often appear novel to children and EAL learners, and their meanings opaque. It is hard for EAL learners to distinguish between literal and non-literal meanings in the formulaic use of such lexical items (see list on page 26).

Talk or written text can be heavily loaded with metaphoric meaning and EAL pupils will often opt out of the struggle to make meaning from them if they are too dense. It is vital though that EAL learners acquire a repertoire of metaphoric

a bolt from the blue	a clean slate
a mountain out of a molehill	a new broom
a red rag to a bull	a turn up for the books
as luck would have it	at sixes and sevens
at the end of the day	be prepared
be that as it may	can I pick your brains
can I run this by you	can I sleep on it
caught in the act	chance your arm
dead of night	dressed up to the nines
even stevens	face the music
fit the bill	fools rush in...
forget it	forewarned is forearmed
frame yourself	from the word go
get on like a house on fire	get real
get your act together	get your skates on
having a ball	I haven't the faintest idea
I haven't the foggiest notion	I wouldn't have missed it for the world
I'll catch you later	I'll chew it over
I'll get back to you	I'll give it a try/a whirl/ a shot
I'll put it on the back burner	in at the deep end
in for a penny, in for a pound	in one fell swoop
it goes without saying	it must be my lucky day
it'll all come out in the wash	it'll be right
just my luck	last but not least
off the hook	light at the end of the tunnel
look before you leap	look lively
look sharp	luck of the devil
miles away	never say die
no chance	not a hope in hell
once in a blue moon	one to one
out of the frying pan into the fire	over the top
paint the town red	people in glass houses
pinch of salt	pull the wool over your eyes
rock bottom	run of the mill
scared stiff	scot free
scream blue murder	see how it turns out
set the ball rolling	seventh heaven
shape up	sit tight
slim chance	smooth operation
storm in a teacup	straight as a die
that's the way it goes	The bee's knees
the missing link	too big for his boots
too good to be true	top brass
true to life	truth will out
turn over a new leaf	water off a duck's back
week in week out	when all's said and done
with a fine tooth comb	worse things happen at sea
you never know your luck	your guess is as good as mine

expression in idiomatic and literary English, and their teacher may be the only person who can unpack the idioms and metaphors they can't understand. Shared imaging of the literal/figurative alternatives of expressions we use unconsciously is a good way to train EAL learners to be alert to figurative meaning and miming – and drawing them can be fun:

> Housework is a pain in the neck. It's like trying to hold back the tide. Last Saturday I threatened the kids with blue murder 'cos the house was knee-deep in junk. It was driving me up the wall. And it wasn't until I really cracked the whip that we got anywhere near ship-shape. They dragged their feet so much I was worn out with the effort of making them play ball. I was a wet rag at the end of the day.

How we store these 'chunks' in our mental lexicon is a question many psychologists continue to explore, but it is clear that a speaker's fluency and range of expression depends on ready access to a large number of these lexical units. Their 'chunking' behaviour makes them economical to use and to comprehend without paying conscious attention to their internal structure, though they do catch our attention when they're used in novel ways, by children or adults:

'set the seeds in motion'

'don't bank all your chickens in one basket'

Figurative expression becomes more opaque when it operates as metonymy, i.e. when a part or component is used to represent the whole:

– we'd have been here half an hour ago if we hadn't been following *a flat cap* all the way from Abergaveny to Brecon.

– that's a nice *set of wheels*.

– not a whisper (of news)

– she's a scream!

Phrasal verbs

Common verbs such as *turn; knock; give* acquire multiple meanings when, as **phrasal verbs** they occur with different prepositions:

turn on	turn off
turn up	turn in
turn out	turn about
turn over	turn under
turn aside	turn down
knock on	knock off
knock up	knock in
knock out	knock about
knock over	knock under
knock aside	knock down

The importance of phrasal verbs in EAL learning is recognised in many FL course-books and syllabuses for students from overseas and is potentially a fruitful area of overlap between FL pedagogy and EAL teaching which teachers of young children need to attend to. The *Collins Cobuild Dictionary of Phrasal Verbs* (1989) provides a lucid rationale for its framework:

> It is often said that phrasal verbs tend to be rather 'colloquial' or 'informal' and more appropriate to spoken English than written, and even that it is better to avoid them and choose single-word equivalents or synonyms instead. Yet in many cases phrasal verbs and their synonyms have different ranges of use, meaning, or collocation, so that a single word synonym cannot be substituted appropriately for a phrasal verb. Single-word synonyms are often much more formal in style than phrasal verbs, so that they seem out of place in many contexts, and students using them run the risk of sounding pompous or just unnatural. (Sinclair, J. and Moon, R. (eds) 1989: iii)

This rationale is aimed at teachers and (older) students of EFL. I believe that young EAL learners in UK classrooms can profit greatly from focused attention to phrasal verbs and their 'formal' synonyms and explore this idea later in the book.

Sinclair and Moon outline four ways in which common English verbs may be combined with adverbial or prepositional particles:

1. combinations where the meaning of the whole cannot be understood by knowing the meaning of the individual verbs and particles. Examples are *go off* (= 'explode'), *put off* (= 'postpone'), and *turn down* (= 'reject').

2. combinations where the verb is always used with a particular preposition or adverb... Examples are *refer to* and *rely on*..

3. combinations where the particle does not change the meaning of the verb, but is used to suggest that the action described by the verb is performed thoroughly, completely or continually. For example in *spread out*, the verb *spread* has its basic meaning, and the adverb *out* adds ideas of direction and thoroughness... in *slave away* and *slog away*, the particle away adds an idea of continuousness to the idea of hard work.

4. ... common verbs which occur in a large number of combinations with different particles, and which have many non-transparent meanings [literal and non-literal] The thirty-eight verbs are:

break	fall	kick	make	put	stay
bring	get	knock	move	run	stick
call	give	lay	pass	send	take
cast	go	lie	play	set	talk
come	hang	live	pull	sit	throw
cut	hold	look	push	stand	turn
do	keep				

(*Source*: Sinclair, J. and Moon, R., 1989: v-vi).

Choices that speakers and writers make between phrasal verbs and single-word synonyms are very often made, consciously or unconsciously, on the basis of style and intended communicative effect. Phrasal verbs can affect the whole 'tone' of longer utterances:

what happened last night?	what are you doing?
how did you get on last night?	what are you playing at?
how did it go last night?	what are you up to?

Appreciation and command of style in oracy and literacy – formal, informal, colloquial, intimate etc. – is part of a prolonged process of linguistic development for all children and requires extensive and specific teaching input. We can make choices in our utterances which have varied communicative effect. For EAL learners this is one of the areas of L_2 development that benefit from reference to L_1 so that differences of cultural mores may be examined. Matching English paired lexical items like *give in – surrender*; *cut down – reduce*; *hang on – wait* with L_1 equivalents helps to develop children's consciousness of communicative effect for different aims and different audiences. Here again shared imaging in the classroom – by describing, miming, simulating or drawing the distinctions of meanings and cultural connotations that each lexical pair evokes – can be the means of crossing language barriers, allowing teachers who do not share pupils' home languages still to promote this inter-lingual word-meaning exploration.

Synonymy

Whether there is such a thing as a 'true' synonym is a much-debated issue in linguistics. A widely held view is that if two words in a language are completely interchangeable then one of them will in the course of time become obsolete. However, many words may be called 'near synonyms' (Lyons, 1995) and these are the basis of most thesaurus listings. Lyons (1995) insists on the importance of not confusing near-synonyms with partial synonyms:

Standard dictionaries of English treat the adjectives 'big' and 'large' as polysemous (though they vary in the number of meanings that they assign to each). In one of their meanings, exemplified by

'They live in a big/large house'

the two words would generally be regarded as synonymous. It is easy to show, however, that 'big' and 'large' are not synonymous in all their meanings... and so are only partially, not absolutely, synonymous. The following sentence,

'I will tell my big sister',

is lexically ambiguous, by virtue of the polysemy of 'big' [older], in a way that

'I will tell my large sister'

is not. ...[This] shows that 'big' has at least one meaning which it does not share with 'large'.

(Lyons, 1995: 61-62)

Not only are the range of meanings for the two words different, the collocation 'large sister' is decidedly unidiomatic.

Synonyms occupy primary teachers and teachers of English a good deal. Instead of accepting 'dull' words like *went, sat, told, walked, good, hard* we exhort children to use *journeyed, slumped, exclaimed, strolled, pleasing*, and *demanding*. EAL pupils often settle for the 'dull' words because they are safe (and easier to spell). Synonyms will be more extensively acquired through literacy experience and this is one reason why we look for story material which provides a rich range of verbs and adjectives, where the meanings of words like *journeyed, slumped, exclaimed, strolled, pleasing*, and *demanding* are contextualised. By consciously targeting such lexical items we can further explore them through actions and role-play and compare them with alternative thesaurus entries.

Antonymy, more commonly called 'opposites', needs attention in the same way as synonymy. Young children prefer *big-small* to *tall-short* and *wide-narrow*, probably because *tall-short* and *wide-narrow* are of higher order visual interpretation. EAL pupils may settle for *big-small* for too long. Sutton's (1992) concern about language in primary science investigations applies also to other investigative and interpretative learning tasks. Lexical pairs such as *strong/weak* as of a bridge; *strong/light* as of wind; *strong/faint* as of a smell, need exploring with reference to L$_1$ for EAL pupils to discover their 'sense', their connotations and their likely collocations.

Gradation or **scale** provides another kind of semantic relationship for grouping and differentiating verbs, adverbs, and adjectives. Warn your colleagues if you want children to work on exploring the meanings of words that make scales beginning with *whisper* and ending with *bellow*; beginning with *whimper* and ending with *howl*; beginning with *bone-dry* and ending with *sopping wet*.

Quite young children are capable of discussing the best words for the three Billy Goats Gruff [small, middle-sized, big or tiny, medium-sized, huge], for Mr Gumpy's car [old, decrepit, ancient], for the Enormous Crocodile, etc. Older children can use thesauri to build scales that start from an adjective or noun they have used in their own writing and then set the task for their classmates to do. And this can work well as a whole class activity, the teacher modelling use of the thesaurus and using the blackboard, flip-chart or overhead projector. (More about these activities and resources in Chapter Five.)

Connotative meaning

One controversy about word-meaning centres around the idea of mental images that we might store for each word, the so-called early 20th century 'snapshot' theory, now largely replaced in theoretical linguistics. But the idea persists that we all hold a number of word-meanings which are strongly associated with one very specific incident or place that is personally memorable so that the meaning for that word is inseparable from the ideas we attach to it idiosyncratically. My daughter delved into the back of the fridge last week and found a piece of mouldy cheese. 'Yuk, it's done a Glasbury!' Every household has words and expressions like this which mean nothing to non-family members but which are loaded with associations for the family.

Other words are loaded with images which are culturally generated i.e. which collectively accrue to words through the patterned experience of communities. Spend a few minutes listing the multi-sensory images you have attached to each of these words:

> *home*   *holiday*   *wedding*

Now test out your lists against a couple of friends or colleagues whose experiences, as you perceive them, differ culturally from your own. In some respects you may be surprised to find how similar your associated images are, in other respects you will hear about things you expected to be different, but did not really appreciate in detail. What you are doing here is constructing a fuller set of meanings for each word which accommodates patterns of cultural experience wider than your own. You are extending imaging to other contexts to enlarge the 'meaning cluster' of each lexical item.

You may go to a dictionary to find a **definition** or **denotative meaning** for each word but the colours, the scents, the music, the sensual, the funny associations which are so importantly part of the cultural meaning of each word are not stored in dictionaries. We might call the collection of images that we associated with each of these words their **connotative** (or **connotational**) **meanings**.

Try a quick 'word association' activity with words which occur frequently in school activities and stories:

bell   *paint*   *wolf*

There are many more 'easy words' to which EAL learners quickly attach denotative meaning and match with L_1 lexicon – but we want them to do more than that. We want them to attach a rich set of cultural connotations to each word because, if their command of the word is limited to specific denotative instances, they will not be alert to the word's meaning potential.

Polemics about the nature of word meaning will probably persist for as long as we struggle to understand human nature or culture or language itself. While the battle rages on among academic giants, we are at liberty to plunder the fruits of their skirmishes and stock our classrooms with a sparkling array of lexical know-how. Although teachers have always 'known' that vocabulary is an important dimension of language learning, the insights of theoretical semantics has not been much exploited in multilingual classrooms. Perhaps because it has all seemed too far removed from curriculum learning, the business of lexical meaning has been overlooked. The gap between practice in multilingual classrooms and theoretical linguistics is all the more regrettable when we acknowledge the natural human propensity to enjoy word-meaning exploration and the relationship between language learning and cognitive growth. The next chapter looks at the development of lexicon in childhood and identifies key features which mirror the theoretical descriptions of lexical behaviours.

Notes and References

1   Formal Welsh-English and Gaelic-English bilingual education are not specific concerns here but Welsh-English and Gaelic-English varieties of bilingualism are implicitly included in the ideas for lexical development In UK classrooms where the language of instruction is not English.

2   The term 'English as an Additional Language' is gaining currency in recognition of the characteristics which predominate in UK multi-ethnic conurbations. The School Curriculum and Assessment Authority (1995) promoted this term at a recent conference:

> The name of the conference emphasised SCAA's intention to take a fresh look at the problems and issues surrounding the education of pupils who are in the process of learning English on entry to school. These pupils already speak another language or languages, and may also be literate in one or more languages. For them, English is an additional language (EAL). There are often more than two languages in use in their home backgrounds, making the description 'English as a second language' (ESL, E2L) not necessarily an accurate one. Despite the presence of languages other than English in pupils' home backgrounds, it is not always the case that these pupils are 'bilingual'. For all of these reasons the descriptive term 'EAL' has been adopted.

(Invitational Conference on Teaching and Learning English as an Additional Language: Conference Papers. London, UK: SCAA Publications.

3   KAL – This term gained currency through the LINC (Language in the National Curriculum) project. Although the findings of the project fell victim to prevalent narrowness of perspectives a good range of its ideas are reported in Carter, 1990.

4   Thank you to Maggie Power and to B.Ed students for these examples.

5   Thank you to B.Ed students for these examples.

6   Thanks again, Maggie!

Chapter Two

Words for learners

> The lexicon is basic to language and language use. It provides the context for syntax and the instantiation of syntactic rules, and it is the environment for phonological and morphological patterns. So understanding what it means to learn a word is critical to the construction of a general theory of how children acquire a language. (Clark, 1993: 259)

Successful development of lexicon in EAL by young children displays broadly the same features that we can discern in first language acquisition. Older children who are at early stages of learning English as an additional language can be seen to operate in patterns similar to younger learners, though they display differences in semantic knowledge and communicative strategies. Knowing how the healthy development of L_2 lexicon mirrors the development of L_1 and knowing in what other respects it differs can indicate when features of lexical behaviour are delayed or absent in L_2 performance. Such knowledge generates an alertness to the differences in experiences between EAL children and their English mother-tongue peers and can help teachers to plan vocabulary-building work in multilingual classrooms.

Proficiency in L_1 is a sound foundation for proficiency in L_2 and research has convincingly shown that children benefit greatly from a richly developed L_1 lexicon – whether that be English or another language. Teachers who share another language with their pupils will recognise that the features of lexical development that this chapter describes for English can also be found in other languages. This is not a matter of 'translation' of English words, but a way of seeing that the same lexical behaviours – polysemy, synonymy, collocation etc. – are present in the way each language works. The more children's semantic control of these behaviours is developed in L_1, the better they will be able to operate with them in an additional language.

The idea of a *lexicon* is as much a theoretical construct as other frameworks that the cognitive sciences propose about child development. The idea suffers somewhat from an understandable tendency to compare the mental lexicon with a written dictionary or a thesaurus – as though our store of words is a measurable and manageable artefact. Neurological science may well one day prove that there is some reality in this, but it is clear from patterns of human language usage that there is more to vocabulary than the words themselves. Lyons (1995) proposes in one of his authoritative studies:

> Looked at from a psychological point of view, the lexicon is the set (or network) of all the lexemes in a language, stored in the brains of competent speakers, with all the linguistic information for each lexeme that is required for the production and interpretation of the sentences of the language. (1995: 73)

Beginners

One of the first and most important cognitive/linguistic steps is for the infant to sort out what a word is. Words or 'word chunks' are what we need firstly and predominantly in communicating, in both L_1 and L_2 acquisition. So beginners in L_1 and L_2 have to discover the words that make up units of meaning. Babies soon get started on the task of sorting out matches of word-forms/meanings and they have a fair amount of it worked out before they begin to produce spoken words of their own, responding in a variety of non-verbal ways to lexical units which have high salience for them.

Studies of mothers and babies show patterns of interaction with strong similarities the world over (Clark 1993), though cultural variations are significant (types of toys, books, opportunities to experiment, take risks, having different carers etc. (Lee and Gupta 1995)). The most significant commonalities of adult-baby verbal interaction seem to be:

- lots and lots and lots of **repetition** – much of it formulaic and routinised

- the lexical meaning is **highly contextualised** – i.e. words are accompanied by actions and immediate concrete objects that have high salience for the child

- a **limited range of semantic fields** – i.e. life revolves around food, toys, body, clothing, washing, the house, shops, the car ...

- familiar **voice patterns** – of adults and older siblings. Articulation plays a role here, but that is not to say that any accent or style of enunciation is more or less difficult for infants: it is the consistency which matters

- a high level of individual **attention and intimacy**, with words and e.g. hand play/peepo

- constant **encouragement**, smiles and cuddles and praise at signs of under-standing.

And most striking:

– the language of people talking to babies is **adapted** according to how the speaker intuitively accommodates to the child. This varies of course, with different cultural patterns, individual inclination of adults and maturation stages of the children.

Remember, all this is the desired and largely normal scenario. There are children whose early experiences lack some of these factors and nursery teachers know some of the signs to look for in such cases. A recent study reveals some evidence that numbers of very small children are missing out because TV tends to distract their mothers' attention, affecting the nature of mother/child talk. At best, television is a stimulus of shared ideas between young children and adults; at worst, it can become a substitute for the natural patterns of contextualised human language essential to the child. By and large, this combination of inter-actions works pretty well for the young L_1 learner. These factors are noteworthy for all teachers of EAL pupils, from nursery right up the school age-range and for teachers who do and teachers who do not share their pupils' mother-tongue. What is important to recognise is the very *human-ness* of this kind of interaction with babies and, as we shall see, with older children. The fact that it is so *instinctive* makes it a double-edged sword. It is the sort of approach which we can slip into with young EAL pupils, without conscious analysis, because teachers are, after all, human. And, by and large, it is a set of strategies based on sound intuition. When learning something complex we all need things to be repeated clearly and comprehensibly, and all of us learn better by being encouraged and praised.

Although this is the generally desired scenario for babies, whether they are at this early stage encountering one or more than one language, it is not wholly sufficient for the cognitive and linguistic development of children of nursery+ ages and it is certainly not sufficient for children accessing the curriculum through EAL. When we trot out the cliché that all teachers are language teachers, what we mean is that all teachers need to be *analytical* language teachers. And it is worth acknowledging a syndrome that bedevils teaching – the belief that just because we all use language, we know all we need to know about teaching it. This folk wisdom can be particularly misplaced when adults who share the home language of EAL pupils are *ipso facto* expected to have theoretical insights into that language. It is an unfair assumption that untrained native speakers (of English or any other language) can automatically apply analytical linguistic knowledge.

Communicative strategies and lexical meaning

It is important to be aware of the distinction between *communication* and *lexical operation*. We communicate by drawing on much more than our knowledge of words. Good communicators do not always have a great vocabulary – in whatever language – an area that has been looked at, *inter alia*, by Labov (1969), Cummins (1984), Saville-Troike (1984) and Hammerley (1991). It is a distinction which we can become less aware of as children become more skilled at communicating.. Bialystock (1990) observes that 'second language learners solve communication problems with remarkable consistency' and expands on a set of strategies which L_2 learners employ to compensate for words they are not able to produce during an utterance. Teachers who are alert to such strategies may also be alert to the lexical gaps which a speaker (or writer) is covering. L_2 (and also L_1) speakers, for example, will often use an **approximation** of the 'missing' word or phrase, or they may use **circumlocution** to avoid need for it. Teachers of EAL pupils will recognise this pattern of compensation for 'missing' English vocabulary. Bialystock (1990) categorises communication strategies as:

- avoidance (message abandonment)

- paraphrase (approximation, word-coinage, circumlocution); – transfer (language switch)

- appeal for assistance.

The pattern of compensatory strategies can be consolidated if the propensity of interlocutors in the multilingual classroom is to *accommodate* to speakers' performance by paying more attention to the ideas content than to the lexical form of utterances. This propensity to accommodate can be particularly pervasive in classrooms where there is a small minority of native English speakers or where the teacher (whether monolingual or bilingual) is the only English-speaker model. Things move fast in the classroom and it is natural to communicate economically, so teachers are right to encourage EAL pupils by responding to their ideas rather than inhibiting them by over much correction, particularly in speech. But just as busy teachers 'accommodate' young learners, so do EAL pupils adapt their performance to the conventions of the classroom and many children consciously or unconsciously conspire to keep busy in ways which mask lexical gaps.

Bialystock (1990) found that circumlocution (when, for example, children describe something instead of naming it) accounted for 80% of strategies she recorded in a study of nine-year old L_2 learners.[1] Whilst some of these instances may have been prompted by grammatical short-comings, I would surmise that the main triggers for circumlocution are lexical gaps. Given a comfortable ethos children are much less bothered than adults by a shaky command of L_2 grammar.

Their concern is with the lexical units that carry the ideas of an utterance – the 'content' words. Circumlocution by EAL pupils is most likely to be due to word shortage. Faerch and Kasper (1983:81) make finer distinctions of some of the categories used above: substitution of one item for another; generalisation for an unknown word (*animal* for *rabbit*); description ('the thing to cook water' in for *kettle*). The 'generalisation' strategy points to the issue of how lexical gaps may affect EAL pupils **categorisation skills**, and I will discuss this in more detail.

Alongside this collection of strategies to compensate for lexical gaps in an additional language, it is worth setting a profile of strategies which serve the communicative functions of speech. Joan Tough (1979) and colleagues identified seven categories (not of linear development) in young children's speech acts. They are reproduced here in the table on page 40.

By matching these categories[2] of communicative functions with the vocabulary appropriate to the contexts of the utterances, we can identify clusters of 'key words' (collocations of lexical items) which teachers may expect or wish children to employ, and we are in a good position to notice whether or not the appropriate lexical items are used. In order to do this we have to envisage a scenario – a location and event – which gives rise to communication. For example, in Tough's 'self-maintaining' category, a child may need words and phrases to express their preference for water rather than milk, and we can in some measure predict the key nouns, verbs, adjectives and adverbs that will be needed; in the 'reasoning' category the child may need to explain how she designed a waterproof container and the teacher will be able to note her use of vocabulary. Where the child's use of words is a poor match with the teacher's expectations, clues to their particular difficulties will be evident in the ways they compensate for lexical gaps (Bialystock and Paribakht above), and also of course for lack of grammatical competence. This approach to identifying the vocabulary needed for curriculum activities depends on some preparation and is discussed in Chapter Three.

O'Malley and Chamot (1990) report on a study of foreign language (FL) learning strategies, some of which include:

Elaboration: relating new information to prior knowledge; relating different parts of new information to each other; making meaningful personal associations to information presented.

Imagery: Using mental or actual pictures or visuals to represent information; coded as a separate category [of cognitive strategy] but viewed as a form of elaboration.

Transfer: Using previously acquired linguistic knowledge to facilitate a language task.

Uses of language and supporting strategies

1. Self-maintaining and group maintaining

Strategies

1. Referring to physical and psychological needs and wants of the self or the groups.

2. Protecting the self or group and self or group interests.

3. Justifying behaviour or claims of self or group.

4. Criticising others.

5. Threatening others.

6. Asserting superiority of self or group.

2. Directing

Strategies

1. Monitoring own actions.

2. Directing the actions of the self.

3. Directing the actions of others.

4. Collaborating in action with others.

3. Reporting on present or past experiences

Strategies

1. Labelling the components of the scene.

2. Referring to detail (e.g. size, colour and other attributes).

3. Referring to incidents.

4. Referring to the sequence of events.

5. Making comparisons.

6. Recognising related aspects.

7. Making an analysis using several features of the above.

8. Extracting or recognising the central meaning.

9. Reflecting on the meaning of experiences, including own feelings.

4. Reasoning

Strategies

1. Explaining.

2. Recognising causal and dependent relationships.

3. Recognising problems and their solutions.

4. Justifying judgements and actions.

5. Reflecting on events and drawing conclusions.

6. Recognising principles.

5. Predicting*

Strategies

1. Anticipating and forecasting events.

2. Anticipating and detail of events.

3. Anticipating a sequence of events.

4. Anticipating problems and possible solutions.

5. Anticipating and recognising alternative courses of action.

6. Predicting the consequences of actions or events.

6. Projecting*

Strategies

1. Projecting into the experiences of others.

2. Projecting into the feelings of others.

3. Projecting into the reactions of others.

4. Projecting into situations never experienced.

7. Imagining*

Strategies

1. Developing an imaginary situation based on real life.

2. Developing an imaginary situation based on fantasy.

3. Developing an original story.

* Strategies which serve *directing, reporting* and *reasoning* may serve these uses also.

Source: Tough, J. *Talk for Teaching and Learning* (1979:36).

Inferencing: Using available information to guess the meanings or usage of unfamiliar language items associated with a language task, to predict outcomes, or fill in missing information (O'Malley and Chamot, 1990).

O'Malley and Chamot affirm the propensities of more effective learners to learners to apply a greater range of strategies:

> Among the cognitive strategies, elaboration emerged as a major learning strategy that was used in a variety of ways, sometimes in combination with other strategies. Elaboration co-occurred with strategies such as imagery, inferencing, and transfer with sufficient regularity to suggest that these strategies may be so closely related as to be inseparable (1990: 139).

Context and meaning

An important aspect of any communication activity is the way in which language may be understood in context. Language made meaningful by non-verbal contextualisation e.g. actions, pictures, 'hands-on' involvement, is more easily comprehensible for EAL learners than language which is decontextualised. For example, the rules of handball are more easily understood by playing the game than by just talking about them; the story of the Three Billy Goats Gruff is made easier to follow if puppets are used. Jim Cummins has been one of the most influential proponents of the need to be aware of different types of linguistic proficiency and the effects of contextualisation on language learning. Cummins (1984) provides a framework which proposes that L_2 learners best acquire new language and new (cognitively demanding) concepts when those concepts and the language which accompanies them are made understandable by the context in which they are embedded. In other words, L_2 learners need the here-and-now characteristic of early L_1 acquisition, that is, when words and phrases occur in familiar routines and are closely matched to concrete objects and actions.

Many foreign language (FL) syllabuses begin with this kind of approach, using role-play in, for example, a scenario such as buying stamps in the post office. The learner quickly understands the meanings of words used to label the most salient objects on the post office counter, and the meanings of phrases used to accompany simple processes such as counting or weighing. However, if the learner is to be able to recognise, retain, and re-use the new language confidently, they need further encounters with the FL words and phrases in 'context reduced' situations where they do not depend on the scenario, and where they can access the meanings directly from the words and phrases themselves – in spoken or written forms. Applying the Cummins framework (page 42) to a structured approach to teaching 'post-office language' in FL classrooms would aim to move the learner from the contextualisation of role-play (as at B in the diagram below) to a point where learners are able to use the language (as at point C below) without the 'props' in speaking or writing.

The FL learner though usually has one great advantage over our youngest EAL pupils. Their learning of the target language is based on prior knowledge of the world. Although post-office routines vary in different countries, once we have learned one variation we have a strong conceptual foundation upon which to pin others. The FL learner has a fully internalised set of concepts about the function of postage stamps, about money, and about the arithmetic of buying stamps, and all they have to do is acquire a new set of words and phrases to accompany concepts which are not of themselves 'cognitively demanding' for them. The cognitive demands on the FL learner come from the need to memorise the new lexical items, and their 'pathway' on Cummins' grid is likely to involve them in rehearsing the use of the new vocabulary, applying mnemonics, etc.

The young EAL learner, on the other hand, has not only new language to learn, they also have new concepts to learn, often at the same time in curriculum contexts. For the young EAL learner, successful understanding of the ideas content and successful acquisition of the new language is best built not on an abrupt move from point B to point C, but on a 'pathway' from point B through progressively stages of decontextualisation to point C. The ideal pathway will be a linked set of activities in which the language is much repeated, and then gradually freed from its embedded usage. Once the words and phrases are confidently internalised the learner is better able to pay attention to the concepts that are being communicated through the words.

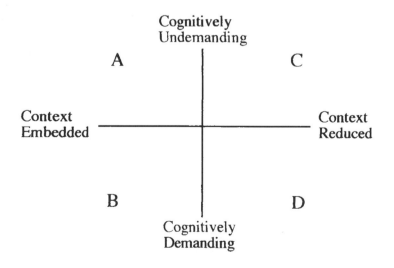

Source: Cummins, J. (1984:139)

Children's command of EAL needs to match those of English mother-tongue speakers for full academic achievement, and inter-personal fluency must not be confused with command of EAL for cognitively demanding situations. As a rule of thumb (but see Collier 1987 and 1988 for age and other affective factors), everyday fluency in EAL is reached by young EAL learners in two years or so of regular exposure, whereas there is an average expectation of peer-appropriate academic linguistic proficiency after about seven years of appropriate input. The big problem that EAL pupils have is time. Even as they continue to develop target language (TL) skills they have to follow the curriculum at the same rate as their English mother-tongue peers. For EAL pupils there needs to be specific input, not only to ensure that they are 'keeping up' with curriculum content but also to train them in conscious linguistic strategies. Just as acrobats need high quality nutrition and careful programmes of exercise to develop their agility, so EAL pupils need to develop the *semantic agility* of successful learners.

In mother-tongue acquisition we can readily see how the contextualisation of linguistic meaning is built into the routines of everyday social encounters. Cummins (1984) acknowledges the influence of Margaret Donaldson (1978) in the development of his theoretical framework for bilingual children's experience:

> She points out that young children's early thought processes and use of language develop within a 'flow of meaningful context' in which the logic of words is subjugated to perception of the speaker's intentions and salient features of the situation. Thus, children's (and adults') normal productive speech is embedded within a context of fairly immediate goals, intentions, and familiar patterns of events. However, thinking and language that move beyond the bounds of meaningful interpersonal context make entirely different demands on the individual, in that it is necessary to focus on the linguistic forms themselves for meaning rather than on the intentions (1984: 140).

Children are expected to comprehend increasingly complex language spoken by the teacher in the classroom. They may appear to have full command of English because they have had a lot of opportunities to direct their own use of spoken language in supportive circumstances. As Donaldson (1978) says:

> When you produce language, you are in control, you need only talk about what you choose to talk about... But this is no longer necessarily true when [the child] becomes the listener. (1978: 73)

Crudely put, the danger in becoming a listener is that EAL pupils may relax into a passive mode of receptivity and lose the propensity to engage actively with the ideas that are being dealt with. Activity-based learning, on the other hand, may fill the day, not allowing time to pay attention to the ways in which the subject matter is being delivered – i.e. to pay attention to the spoken and written words which convey the meanings.

'Labelling, packaging and network-building'

What then is the work that young children do in developing a lexicon? I find it illuminating to take Jean Aitchison's idea that 'children are faced with three different but related tasks – **a labelling task, a packaging task and a network-building task'** (Aitchison, 1987) and to look at these tasks for relevance to L_2 acquisition at different ages.

Firstly, **labelling**. Sequences of sounds can be used as names for things and this is most obvious in labels like *Jackie, Jamilla, Joshua* where the label 'belongs' to one entity. For all the thousands of Jackies, Jamillas, Joshuas we know exist, as far as a small child is concerned *Jackie*, or *Jamilla*, or *Joshua* 'denotes' one person. Aitchison (1987:87) reminds us though, that the realisation that bits of sound 'mean' an object/person comes at age one to two – *after* children produce their first utterances. Early vocalisations produced by small children in response to something like a pet or a cup, are more likely to be ritual responses in oft-repeated activities, rather than symbolic use of words:

> The ability to symbolise emerges slowly, then. It may be innate, in the sense that it may be biologically programmed to develop some time before the age of two, as long as the child is provided with a normal environment. But it is unlikely that a new-born baby or a child under one year realises that the sounds that come out of people's mouths 'stand for' things and actions. This shows that in studying the mental lexicon, we must be quite sure that children are truly labelling things before we start to draw conclusions from their behaviour (Aitchison, 1987:89).

By using **contextual clues** children are able to behave as though they are responding to words before they make the connections between words and the things words refer to (referents), and respond to repeated 'formulaic' phrases, particularly if the intonation and stress patterns of these are consistent:

> Mothers often feel that their one-year-olds understand everything that is said to them. The child uses all the available contextual clues such as the parents' gesture and intonation, and his familiarity with the situation to interpret what is going on. In fact, the child understands few of the actual words, and perceives them merely as part of the total situation. For example, if a mother asks her child to sit down for dinner while pulling out the highchair and tying on his bib as food smells waft from the kitchen, he would be unlikely not to understand what she wanted (Cooke and Williams, 1985: 7).

Gradually the child recognises key words in these routine phrases, so that *cup* becomes associated with a collection of actions (getting the orange juice, then drinking) and eventually with the object itself (Reynell, 1980). There is a stage, therefore, in which *cup* has meaning through use, rather than as a true linguistic symbol for the object.

The words children learn to understand and eventually produce are closely related to their daily routines and are therefore culturally determined. Vocabulary reflects the most salient factors of the child's environment: food, clothes, washing, household objects and toys and other names of people. EAL pupils of nursery age or older do not repeat the major cognitive step of their mother-tongue acquisition in understanding that words 'stand for' (symbolise) things and actions, but they do repeat the behaviour of reproducing English words and phrases that are spoken to them and also respond in ways which may appear to contain understanding when in fact they are using cues from other sources, e.g. copying other children's actions. This mode of repeating and responding without understanding the meaning of some words and phrases can persist for quite a long time and overlaps with genuine understanding and response to other words and phrases. First indications of understanding are responses to English in ways which show understanding but without verbalising. The speaker (teacher) will typically behave as though the learner understands, as in L_1 mother talk. The child becomes more able and willing to reproduce teacher words, especially when they are carefully articulated by the teacher. At this stage the child is still adjusting to English speech characteristics (phonetic qualities), responding to questions/commands with one word, usually the last word of English utterance (in simple English patterns this is usually the most salient part of the sentence) e.g. What's your name? Hang up your coat. Sit on the carpet. For the child very new to English, much repetition over a period of time is needed to isolate the words that carry the most force in the utterance. Here the young EAL child has an environmental advantage over older EAL beginners. Life in the nursery is very routinised and actions are regularly accompanied by the same formulaic instructions and observations, so that word meanings are highly contextualised.

Single words and short phrases are produced first and used by the learner to label people and concrete objects. Single words (nouns, verbs, nominals) are also used effectively to convey a wide range of concepts – *paint painting*, and since the child has already a highly developed range of instrumental L_1 for expressing needs and wants, organising people, commenting on the world and so on, these functions are quickly transferred to English. Single words are used to do more than label, as in stating ownership or location when the L_1 child might point to shoes while saying *mummy*; or look in a cupboard and say, 'cup'. This then extends to two-word utterances *mummy cup* and this can 'mean' many different things. While these two word utterances in L_1 signal the beginnings of grammar and serve the young child's needs well with the willing cooperation of adults who know them intimately, the same behaviour in EAL – *miss paintbrush*, is used to cope in a very different milieu for more complex intentions, as for example using words to express category membership, to express perceptual or functional similarity, as a means of drawing attention to something about the world or some event (Clark 1993:34). **Holophrases** (single words doing the work of whole sentences) can persist and in the busy classroom among L₁ speakers, a child can manage very well with a small number of salient words and expressions.

Formulas (whole chunks, unanalysed routines) are often indistinguishable from single words *off-to-bed have-a-drink*. Formulas are an important part of linguistic performance and some people (see Ellis 1994:84-88) claim that we use thousands of them in everyday speech: *come in, how are you? do take a seat, I won't be a moment, sorry to keep you waiting...* etc. These more 'literal' formulas are as important to us as the more figurative expressions I illustrated in Chapter One. The two kinds of formulas make up a surprisingly high proportion of our everyday speech. Children will use formulas as unanalysed chunks for some time and then break them up into parts to use as patterns: *I wanna, gimiya, I gota* etc. in more extended utterances. Spelling errors made by children aged seven and over indicate that word boundaries remain unclear in a lot of expressions like these and continue to be stored and used as chunks without attention to their constituent parts. Others are consciously attended to:

Q. Where did Napoleon keep his army?
A. Up his sleevey

'Nan, what does 'it's a small world' mean?'

The answer to this last question illustrates how adults use formulaic metaphor unconsciously:

'It means you're always bumping into people.'[3]

Use of formulas has significant and long-term implications for EAL pupils' control of English. Bialystock (1991) draws attention to this in her discussion of the contextualised nature of children's conversations:

Children talk about things present, the 'here and now'... conveying and interpreting meanings can be achieved with only casual attention to the language itself.....

Second-language learners frequently manage to reduce the demands for analysis by the use of highly practised and conventionalised 'chunks' or patterns of language... These chunks, then, are treated as meaning units, part of the unanalysed representations of language that are the basis of the system of words and meanings. As these chunks become analysed, they will be used in more creative contexts and be separated into their components' (1991: 126-70).

Persistent lack of analysis of 'chunks', on the other hand reduces control and creativity. Saville-Troike (1984) concludes that attention to form is one of the most significant factors affecting achievement of second language learners. The phonological forms of words are duplicated in homophones and in polysemic words, contributing to the opportunities for mis-comprehension. Children's individual meaning-making is influenced by the things that are important in their lives and the 'images' they store privately for word-meanings are often at odds with those of adults. A student-teacher reports on one instance of a child not able to extend the meaning of polysemous words appropriately in context:

> We were tacking in a sewing activity and when I asked what 'tacking' meant, one girl said it was like tack for horses. 'No,' I said. 'Tacking as in sewing.' 'It must be sewing a picture of a saddle or a horse,' she said.

For this child a personal **connotative meaning** was more salient than the 'here and now' contextualised meaning that the teacher was constructing. This was also the case with the earlier examples of the '*king's taxis*' and the '*apple saws*' (instead of *taxes* and *sauce* as intended by the teachers). Visits to a fabric shop called '*The Shuttle*' continually disappointed my young son who never saw the space-ships he expected to be on sale there. Connotative meaning, whether idiosyncratic or drawn from patterned cultural experiences, may so influence

children's comprehension of lexical items that they simply do not 'hear' the meanings intended by others.

Words for **concrete referents** initially predominate as words for actions are added. These are gradually combined with negation to command and to make observations *don't sit* and other general purpose verbs *do, make, get, go.* 'They are more likely to talk about their own actions ...more likely to talk about movement which is directly observable, than about causes or goals. And their verbs of motion are the first to be extended to talking about the activities of others, followed only later by other verbs.' (Clark, 1993) Older children may continue to use single words to convey a large range of meanings... and this can be accepted too readily as adequate English expression. Deictic terms – *it, that, there, now* (expressing time and place) play a big role in lexical substitution. It takes children much longer to sort out the meanings of many verbs than it does nouns. Eight and a half to ten and a half year-olds were asked to guess the meaning of *lidber* from the sentence 'Jimmy lidbered stamps from all over the world', and they interpreted *lidber* as *collect*. They then interpreted 'The police did not allow the people to lidber on the streets.' as meaning that the police did not allow the people to collect stamps on the street (Werner and Kaplan in Aitchison, 1987). The subjects here, unable to discern the boundaries of lexical

meaning, are misled by the collocation of *collect* and *stamps.* Such examples give us clues as to how young learners may be led into erratic interpretations of adult word usage, when they are unable to over-ride a 'fixated' contextualised meaning.

Learning patterns

In broad stages EAL children will map meanings onto the English words they hear 'for objects, for agents and instruments, for actions and for undoing actions (Clark 1993)' covering the same ideas that they mapped in first language acquisition, and though they do not repeat the very early conceptualisation of these they need time to isolate the English word forms and consolidate their match with L_1 lexicon. They may go through a silent phase, using sub-vocal speech or 'inner rehearsal' as they get underway with this task. Fitzpatrick (1987) cautions the need to observe the behaviour of new learners to decide whether non-response indicates trauma, but notes the potential benefit of this 'listening' phase:

> For the acquisition of basic language skills, the best results seem to be gained from language used naturally, for genuine communicative purposes in contexts which are concrete and support the meanings being communicated in a clear way. For most learners a period of listening to the second language in such contexts appears to be a necessary and fruitful way into the new language which pays off later in better proficiency (Fitzpatrick 1987:97-8).

The young EAL learner soon works out that a non L_1 speaking teacher doesn't understand her and will naturally choose to talk more to a bilingual peer or adult who does. The bilingual teacher can start here to insert English words/phrases in L_1 sentence structures and encourage their production from the child. This will ensure that the child rapidly acquires a repertoire of key words and phrases without stress. Without this mother-tongue support there are plenty of opportunities for ambiguity between interlocutors and frustration on the part of the child. Teachers who are not able to support the child through fluent use of L_1 must expect a variety of reactions by young children to their situation. Frustration is a real and pervasive experience for EAL pupils and we need to regard it seriously. If it is acute and prolonged it can seriously affect a child's personality. Even mild frustration in communicating can inhibit children's motivation and willingness to take risks, and successful learners have to be risk-takers. Older early-stage EAL learners are even more vulnerable when they risk embarrassment or ridicule by peers or even teachers. So adults who are able to use children's L_1 – whether they are limited to a few words or are fully fluent – can powerfully affect their sense of cultural belonging in the classroom and also the other children's attitudes.

When it does begin, production of L_2 vocabulary will expand rapidly in broadly similar patterns to L_1, although to different time scales depending on the motivation engendered by the classroom ethos, teacher skill and individual personality of the learner. There is widespread debate about measures of children's L_1 vocabulary development – largely due to the difficulties of counting polysemes, inflected words, compounds etc. but also because of the practical problems of recording children's total production. Passive vocabulary knowledge, it is generally agreed, always outstrips productive vocabulary, and as estimates are based on perceived comprehension, far from being an exact science, the estimates vary widely. From age 2, children acquire about ten new words per day, so by age six have about 14,000 words (according to Carey, 1978). From age 10-11 children encounter about 10,000 new words per year. 'Between 9-15 they're exposed to 85,000 distinct word roots, at least 100,000 distinct word-meanings in their school textbooks' (Clark, 1990). Estimates of adult English speaker production vocabulary vary between 20,000 and 50,000 word forms; others range from 150,000 to 250,000 words, and comprehension vocabulary of much more is proposed. This information does not really add to our knowledge of L_2 lexical development, but it does give an idea of the enormity of the tasks facing L_2 learners if they are aiming to match the quantity of L_1 lexicon.

In any context that is new to us we will extend our range of labels for real world referents:

> Shock-cord sectioned alloy poles slide into continuous inner sleeves and slot into eyelets. A series of Velcro connections to the flysheet are placed to reinforce the fly guy ropes.

The business of labelling things gets started as soon as children become involved in any kind of equipment – buttons, buckles and poppers on clothing; shower gel, shampoo and shaving cream in the bathroom ... It gets serious when peer grouping centres around activities such as computer games or skate-boarding. Children pay most attention to those words which have high salience for them, whether in L_1 or L_2, but their interpretation of words is also influenced by what is salient for them and, with several things in their heads at any one time, their constructed meaning for words used by teachers can be extraordinarily divergent. Hardy (1997) reports on Year 5 children's understanding of words prior to their use as key terms used in a science topic:

liquid	→ Fairy [washing-up liquid], green, slimy
materials	→ clothes, carpets, wool
solution	→ brain, idea
gas	→ smoke, petrol, fire
separate	→ mums and dads being apart
mixture	→ sweets, cake
filter	→ camera, waggons, pipes

Clark (1993) identifies a number of ontological categories (ways of sorting out knowledge about the world) which young children draw on as they match their own experiences to the words of the language they are learning (as L_1): objects, actions, events, relations, states and properties. Clark proposes that children show strong evidence of forming object categories before they speak by spontaneously touching like objects in sequence, and by matching pictures of like objects. Shape appears to be the chief property by which they will sort objects, and this influences the over-extension of nouns in early lexical production:

Characteristic over-extensions from one- and two-year-olds:

Word	First referent	Successive over-extension
bird	sparrows	cows, dogs, cats, any animal moving
titi	animals	pictures of animals, things that move
tee	cat	dogs, cows and sheep, horse
buti	ball	toy, radish, stone spheres at park entrance
tick-tock	watch	clock, all clocks and watches, gas meter, firehose on spool, bathscale with round dial
ball	rubber ball	apples
bébé	reflection of self	photo of self, all photos, all pictures, all books with pictures, all books
kotibars	bars of cot	large toy abacus, toast rack with parallel bars, pictures of building with columns
fly	fly	specks of dirt, dust, all small insects, own toes, crumbs of bread, toad
pin	pin	crumb, caterpillars
koko	cockerel crowing	tunes on violin, tunes on piano, tunes on accordion, tunes on phonograph, all music, merry-go-round
dany	sound of bell	clock, telephone, doorbells
cola	chocolate	sugar, tarts, grapes, figs, peaches
sizo	scissors	all metal objects
va	plush dog	muffler, cat, father's fur coat

[note: commas separate successive over-extensions]

Source: Clark 1973a, reproduced in Clark 1993.

L₂ learners of school age will have already reached a much more sophisticated stage of categorizing than this, but will nevertheless be restricted in their ability to communicate their ideas in L₂. Working on categorization in L₁ can build on the sound foundations of children's perception of detail and if this is repeated in English they will rapidly acquire the L₂ labels needed for the task. As finer and more subtle detail is needed to differentiate and group objects, so the advantages of using L₁ before transfer into L₂ will be apparent. When the ideas are firmly grasped the L₂ labels will be more rapidly acquired.

Packaging and world knowledge

'**Packaging**' is the second linguistic task in mother-tongue acquisition, described by Aitchison (1987:89) as the child develops realisation that labels can be applied to collections of items. Two things can happen here: **under-extension**, so *dog* is used for big dogs, not for small ones, and **over-extension**, so *dog* is used for all four-legged animals. Again this is a phase which is normally prolonged for mother-tongue speakers. Under-extension can be recognised as a development from situation-bound labelling. Aitchison (1987) reviews examples of under-extension of adjectives: *white* – associated only with snow, not with a blank page; *deep* and *shallow* for a swimming pool, but not for puddles. Three to four-year-olds were happy to call milk *cold*, water *deep*, boxes *hard*, and trees *crooked*, but would not allow that the terms could be applied to people. It may well be that some researchers' judgements of under-extension are confused by use of figurative meanings: *cold, deep, hard* and *crooked* are applied figuratively to people, and we would expect that children's understanding of the polysemous range of meanings attached to such words needs time to develop. We need to remember that native-speakers are prone to unconscious use of metaphor in these apparently 'easy' words.

Over-extension, says Aitchison (1987) is probably less common than under-extension, but more noticeable. Examples include categorical over-inclusion, so *chair* includes sofa, bench, stool and a large stone that you can sit on. Three explanations are considered by Aitchison for over-extension: lack of knowledge, 'mental fog' and wrong analysis – all ideas which teachers of EAL children will recognise as relevant to their pupils:

– lack of knowledge – a small repertoire leads the child to apply the word in a non-adult way, so *horse* might be applied to donkeys, mules and zebra. (Inner-city children can confuse horses and cows.)

– 'mental fog' – meanings/classifications are vague and unimportant to the child. *Horse,* for example, suffices to include animals that are large, have smooth coats and long tails. Other details are added as world knowledge increases and the need for discriminatory terms grows.

    — wrong analysis – In this respect Vygotsky (1934) thought that children are capable of analysis but focus on only one aspect and generalise in ways that do not fit adult patterns. His idea of 'chained complexes' can mystify parents of small children when, for example, *qua* is used for duck on a pond; for cup of milk; for a coin with an eagle on it, and for a teddy bear's eye. The connections lie only in what is salient to the child: the pond water is liquid like the milk; the shape of the cup connects with the roundness of the coin; the eye of the eagle connects with the eye of the teddy bear to make them all quas (Vygotsky in Aitchison, 1987:91-92).

Young EAL pupils will be going through this stage in their first language as well as in English and many studies demonstrate how languages apply labels differently. In the celebrated case of *snow* (see for example Lakoff's discussion, 1987) it might be said by Lapps that English mother-tongue speakers over-extend the term, applying it indiscriminately to that cold, white stuff that comes down from the sky and collects on the ground. (*Slush* and *sleet* and *powder* are scant match for their reputed 22 terms.)

    Speakers of radically different languages may not share all the same basic experiences. Some of these experiences may be acquired by living in the culture where the language is spoken, though living in such a culture as an outsider may well not provide the right kind of experiences to understand all of the concepts of those who have grown up in the culture (Lakoff, 1987: 312).

The process of 'packaging' very quickly leads to the use of words for **classifying** or **categorizing**. Categorization has for many years been regarded by psychologists as one of the fundamental attributes of human cognition. Lee and Gupta (1995) review arguments which lead to a view of categorization as the foundation of conceptual development. We cannot get very far without conceiving of things as sets and without using words to consolidate ideas of sets. It might be said that every noun is a generalisation – we can't use the word *chair* without having a generalised idea of 'chairhood'. Categorization, though, involves us in placing word-meanings in hierarchical relations. For example *bird* is in hierarchical relation to *sparrow* and *lark* and *pigeon*. In this relationship *bird* is a **superordinate** for the **hyponyms** *sparrow*, *lark* and *pigeon*. But these hierarchies of word-meaning change according to our intentions in organising our world knowledge: *bird* in relation to *tiger*, *dragonfly* and *creature* loses its function of superordinate and becomes one of the hyponyms of the superordinate *creature*. Again, *tiger* in relation to *mammal* collects other hyponyms around it such as *whale*, *kangaroo* and *human*. Cultural knowledge endlessly extends our need to categorize:

Children's hierarchical levels of categorisation reflect the salience of objects in their lives: *bird* – is more likely than *sparrow, pigeon*; *liquid* – is less likely to be used than *water, milk, paint*; *footwear* – is less likely to used than *shoe, trainer, slipper*. The L$_2$ vocabulary of categories has to be attended to, because numerous category labels depend on hierarchical schemas and cannot be taken for granted. Ten-year-old EAL pupils were unable to place *furniture* in hierarchical relation to *cupboard*, or *building* in relation to *mill* (McWilliam, 1997).

Categorisation is one aspect of linguistic control which affects cognition and our ability to organise ideas about the world. We cannot function intelligently without sorting objects, actions, events etc. into 'types' or sets that we label or describe or otherwise refer to with words. It is easy for teachers to take for granted that EAL pupils who are interpreting and constructing ideas in English are making the necessary connections between the words used to express categorized ideas (be they objects, actions, events or whatever) and the ideas themselves. For example, *strolling* belongs to the category 'ways of walking'; *chortle* belongs to the category 'types of laugh'.

Classification is built around the idea of 'inclusion'. Thus *boat* is a **superordinate** that includes the idea of *yacht, canoe* and *catamaran*; *food* includes the idea of *pastry, pasta*, and *fruit* – each of which become themselves superordinates to *Danish, flaky, shortcrust* etc.; *cannelloni, lasagne, fetuccini* etc. and so on. Children have to learn these meaning relations in order to understand and use the terms appropriately. We expect them to take several years over doing this, and in fact it is a process that we continue to refine throughout adulthood. How many times have you puzzled over an entry for a household service or a retailer in Yellow Pages? EAL learners, however can miss out on the culturally contextualised occurrences of these 'word families'. They may first meet them in written texts, where their knowledge of them may be taken for granted. Look at categories that our industrial society generates and is defined by (see page 56).

Mental categories and the words we use for them are constantly affected by cultural experience. For example, the English label *bird* is applied to creatures that lay eggs and have feathers and wings, but children's encounters with ducks, chickens, ostriches etc., whether directly or on television, may take place at times when they are operating in home language. *Bird* may then become restricted in use to the more prototypical species – sparrows, pigeons, starlings etc. *Bird* is useful enough in many circumstances but unless the child's understanding of it is extended, its use as a superordinate term (in English) is inhibited. National Curriculum science will eventually attend to such classifications, but many others will be assumed as 'general knowledge'. What we forget is that many instances of classification are culturally determined and do not match neatly across languages. *Dom*, for example translates from Russian and Polish as both *house* and *building*. In many cultures *chicken* is not classed as meat.

KARAOKE
KARTING
KITCHEN PLANNERS and FURNISHERS
KITCHEN WARE
KITES
KNITTING YARN MNFRS and
    WHOLESALERS
KNITWEAR and TEXTILES
LABELS and TAGS
LABORATORY EQUIPMENT|
LACE MAKERS
LADDER SALES
LADIESWEAR – RETAIL
LAMPSHADE MNFRS and DISTRIBUTORS
LANDSCAPE ARCHITECTS andDESIGNERS
LANGUAGE SCHOOLS
LASER EQUIPMENT – SALES, SERVICE and
    REPAIR
LAUNDRIES and LAUNDERETTES
LAUNDRY EQUIPMENT – SALES and
    SERVICE
LAWNMOWERS and GARDEN
    MACHINERY
LEADED LIGHTS AND WINDOWS
LEATHER MERCHANTS and
WHOLESALERS
LEATHER PRODUCTS – MNFRS and
    SUPPLIERS

LEATHERGOODS SHOPS
LEGAL SERVICES
LEISURE and RECREATION CENTRES
LEISURE WEAR
LIBRARIES
LIFE ASSURANCE
LIFT MNFRS
LIFTING EQUIPMENT
LIFTS – SERVICING and REPAIRS
LIGHTING CONSULTANTS
LIGHTING MNFRS
LIGHTING RETAILERS
LIGHTING WHOLESALERS
LINGERIE and HOSIERY – RETAIL
LIST BROKERS
LITHOGRAPHIC PLATE MAKERS
LOANS
LOCKSMITHS
LOFT CONVERSIONS
LOOSE COVERS
LUBRICANT MNFRS and DISTRIBUTORS
LUGGAGE RETAIL and WHOLESALE

*THE THOMSON LOCAL DIRECTORY:
BRADFORD, KEIGHLEY, SKIPTON AREA
1996-97*

It takes longer for children to sort out categories for things in the world which are not countable in the same way as animals and household objects. Sand and water and grass and sky are perhaps not as easy to pick out as things they can discern, and in situations when adults point to these things it can be hard for young children to work out quite what they are referring to when many other eye-catching objects may also be present. Young EAL pupils may likewise overlook **mass nouns** in favour of **count nouns**.

Categories of actions are a good deal hazier than those of objects. Clark (1993) provides a telling example:

> Consider the activities we group together as instances of 'holding'. These include a vase holding flowers; a hand holding a fork, cup, plate, pebble or water; a father holding a baby; a truck holding sand or bricks; a rubber band holding hair, and so on. The range [is] largely determined by how an activity is adapted to each object it affects.

The difficulty of categorizing meanings for verbs in EAL is further exacerbated by the high frequency of **phrasal verbs**, so *hold on, hold up, hold out, hold against* etc. further blur the semantic 'sets' that children have to work out.

Adjectives are used to communicate ideas about the shape, size, colour, composition and quality of objects, and small children perceive a great deal of detail in objects that they encounter (see Clark 1993 for a close study of this). For example, *broken* is used to comment on things which they notice are not quite right – a torn magazine, a blunt pencil, a cracked paving stone. With adult interaction in a variety of contexts L_1 learners will build up a cluster of 'break/broken' words: *tear/torn*; *bust*; *crack/cracked*; *split*; *snap/snapped*; *chip/chipped*; *fracture/fractured*; *splinter* etc. as these occur in **collocation** with objects of differing composition. EAL learners need the same range of encounters so that *break/broken* is not over-extended inappropriately.

Many adjectives are formed from verbs but this connection is not self-evident to children. Bilingual teachers can target L_1 equivalent clusters of verbs and adjectives and verb/adjective pairs so that EAL children are alerted to the range of possible meanings for which they need to acquire English words. These clusters of adjectives and verbs support the argument that there is no such thing as a true synonym and EAL children have a lot of work to do in sorting out the English vocabulary of actions and properties, especially as they are unlikely to match one for one with L_1 lexicon. But children are good at this kind of mental work and are disposed to map meanings onto words quite rapidly. With an alert adult providing plenty of opportunities to check their meanings and receive confirmation or correction in an encouraging manner, children will enthusiastically explore a wide range of lexical items centred around one main idea e.g.: *Break/broken* – see page 58.

Synonymy holds it own fascination for children and they frequently demonstrate spontaneous interest in 'families' of words, long before they are led to study them more formally in school:

a lot of...

a mixture	a combination	a blend
a hotchpotch	a melée	a jumble
a collection	an assortment	a flock
a herd	a clutch	a school
a bale	a pool	a swarm
a congregation		

Adjectives: Broken

cracked plaster

broken windowpane

rusty window frame

frayed cushions

tattered curtains

peeling paintwork

leaky pipe

faded sofa

wilted flowers

torn spine

dusty table top

ripped cover

dog-eared pages

chipped cup

worm-eaten table

threadbare rug

rickety chair

crumpled paper

stained carpet

Longman Contemporary English Dictionary. Reprinted by permission of Addison Wesley-Longman Ltd.

look...

glance	peer	stare
gawp	eye	regard
examine	scrutinise	contemplate

When teaching poetry, the role of synonyms becomes a focus of semantic consciousness. They are the very stuff of poetry, where we strive to encapsulate an idea in verbal form:

How do things move?
elephants lumber, lurch, plod, sway, trudge, tramp, stampede;
water seeps, leaks, trickles, oozes, flows, runs, pours, rushes, pounds;
a cat ....
an insect...........
a ball..............
a lorry.............

Use a thesaurus and a bilingual dictionary to try:

ways of looking/touching/eating/talking...

Children's use of synonyms often has amusing results:

– You look ready for bed, Tommy

– I'm well-prepared

– I saw a man with a roomy dog

– It's on TV every week. It's a serious.

While all this language processing is going on, children are learning about the world and storing information in memory. They continue to map meanings onto words that they encounter according to their experiences of the words in the context of actions and processes as well as concrete objects, and they move on to more complex discrimination of **properties, conditions** and **relations** (Clarke, 1993).

The properties of objects are subject to judgements and comparisons. 'A small elephant is a large animal', said Sapir, demonstrating that how we talk about objects and actions depends very often on how we perceive them in relation to other objects and actions. *Big, small; heavy, light; high, low; fast, slow; near, far* are terms that children have to learn to apply in **scale** or **gradation**, rather than as **binary opposites**. Remember the feeling of being on the very top of the world when you pushed out your feet to take the playground swing as high as you could? Remember the great expanse between you and first base on the rounders pitch? Look at them now! As we grow older (and bigger) and as we learn about the way the world works, we learn to use words which represent the properties of objects, actions and events with more consideration for their relationships with other objects, actions and events – *bigger, smaller; slower, faster; cheaper, more expensive; simple, more complicated* etc.

The known and the unknown

Analogy becomes an important linguistic tool for children to employ in understanding and producing these ideas, especially when they are comparing objects which are not present simultaneously, or actions and events separated in time: 'it's like my chair only bigger'; 'I like these more better than my old shoes'; 'it's further than when we went to Granny's house'. Analogy depends entirely on experience of the world and in communicating ideas young children rely heavily on shared cultural understandings. They unconsciously assume that others are able to 'image' their own personal world until they gradually come to realise that their own cultural experiences differ from those of others and that analogy needs to become part of the business of negotiation of 'shared imaging'. Children entering nursery or reception class need the reassurance that there are connections between their own world and the strange world of school, and all children experience a measure of culture-shock at this stage of major transition. If their language of analogy and their referents – objects, actions and events of home and community culture – are very different from those of their teacher, then it is good deal more difficult to use words to place familiar objects, actions and events in relation to new objects, actions and events. Teachers who share children's home language and cultural mores play a vital role in enabling EAL children to make analogies between home and school in ways which extend relational concepts.

Older EAL pupils are affected by distance of cultural analogy in sustained and pervasive ways. Relations of objects, actions and events are expressed, in all languages, in 'word-chunks' which have the function of communicating culturally generated ideas of their significance. English uses the term **simile** to name the formulaic way that many of these occur – typically using the patterns as...as..., or like... for example, *as quick as lightening; like a bolt from the blue; quick as a flash*; and by **idioms** which are also used as chunks of meaning in natural speech and in story texts: *before I knew where I was...; in the wink of an eye; at the drop of a hat; before you could say Bob's your uncle...* Many EAL children who have reached a stage of surface fluency which serves them well for most common interpersonal communication have absorbed only a limited range of such expressions in English. The figurative nature of many of these lexical units makes their meanings opaque and understanding them requires focused attention.

Whilst all this is a normal pattern for very young L_1 learners, it is important that teachers recognise that the implications for the acquisition of EAL are different. We expect that all this will be going on in children's mother-tongue development and we have to expect that it will extend over a number of years, just as it will for monolingual children. Their world knowledge is increasing rapidly at the same time as all these words are being learned. Ideas differ as to how much correct application of words in these 'packaging tasks' depends on adult-child interaction with usage of terms, or on the child's perception of the features of objects. The task is not concerned purely with physical, observable features. It is complicated by the nature of many words which may be used literally and figuratively, as in the *cold, deep* example, and others which apply to actions rather than objects. Whether adult-child interaction is more or less important than the child's own use of perceptual information is debatable, but what is needed by the child is the vocabulary which must be used to communicate ideas about the objects or actions. For the bilingual child extra terms are needed depending on whether their interaction is with L_1 or English speakers. The quality and quantity of that interaction will affect the range and accuracy of their word usage. Clark reminds us that 'errors' (in L_1) should not be taken *per se* to indicate cognitive problems:

> Children who over-extend words in production typically do not over-extend them in comprehension. That is [they] understand the words they over-extend in production. This would be consistent with over-extension being a communicative strategy: use the nearest word that seems appropriate (Clark, 1993:35).

Target vocabulary for target understanding

For very young EAL pupils labelling/packaging tasks are consistent with the accumulation of vocabulary which nursery teachers expect to have to attend to. However, the frequency of repetition, intimacy and affirmation which is afforded by mothers to their children in early L_1 is rarely possible in school. It may be that the routines, the play, the topics and the story experiences of nursery and reception class provide a *corpus* of English lexical units which serve young EAL learners very well for the demands made on them in the beginning stages of schooling. If, however, bilingual and monolingual staff systematically target L_1 and English nouns, verbs, adjectives and adverbs so that the words are highlighted for the child in the contexts of different activities and so that their attention is repeatedly drawn to the words and their meanings, the children's alertness to word-meanings will be made overt rather than unconsciously pragmatic. If this sounds like training, it is intended to be so, because EAL pupils need an established attitude to words and word meaning.

Clive Sutton (1992) talks about how our understanding of the world around us is affected by our use of language: by its effect on the way we organise (remember) our previous experience, and by its influence on the way we construct theories (belief systems). Words affect the meanings we attribute to sensory perceptions. We use words to organise our seeing, and to organise our memories. We also use words to organise the material world in which we live and the activities in which we engage. Jackendoff (1983) expands on the crucial aspects of categorisation and the effects of word meaning on the way we systematise our world knowledge. He examines the idea of 'prototypes', that is the 'necessary, central and typical' properties of things that make us decide how to group them. Pigeons and ostriches share the same necessary, central and typical characteristics which place them into the category 'birds'. This reminds us to question the cultural assumptions upon which native-speaker discourse is often founded, particularly when we are asking EAL pupils to build concepts on the basis of assumed common knowledge.

Sorting activities are commonly used in UK primary science classrooms to develop multi-sensory perceptions and to extend the language of enquiry which young children need in order to become good investigators. As Sutton (1992) tells us, our use of words can significantly affect our perceptions and the processes in which we engage. In approaching a sorting activity (see the chart opposite, which we have already met in Chapter One) as a semantic activity, learning about materials and their properties can be enhanced.

You might like to involve colleagues in the following activity. You will need a collection of objects or slips of paper with the written names of objects. You will also need thesauri and bilingual dictionaries (see page opposite):

If the children are encouraged to use thesauri to build on 'easy' words like *hard* and *soft* and use synonyms such as *rigid flexible brittle malleable compressible*, their investigations immediately become far more detailed. The quality of their attention to the task is greatly enhanced. They realise that the objective of the lesson is not to complete the task but to maximise the opportunities for genuine learning. More rigorous attention to word-meaning leads to more rigorous enquiry into science ideas.

Lexical units may be highlighted as they occur in a teaching topic. It is the contextualisation of words, whether in story, conversation, instruction, poetry or whatever, which drives the need for attention to them. In order to comprehend and apply words, learners need to be able to attach 'senses' or 'images' to them, to the patterns (utterances) in which they occur, and to the 'script' which provides the context for their occurrence. The script in which words occur will, particularly for younger learners, often be aural/oral, experiential and multi-sensory, if, for example, the teacher is asking children to classify objects

Objects to be sorted into sets according to their physical properties

cardboard box	twig	chalk	paper clip
soft teddy	nail	foil	rubber
stone	plastic pen	marble	glass tumbler
foam	wool	candle	wooden ruler
plasticine	straw	shell	ping pong ball
cork	brass screw	plastic cup	smooth pebble

SORTING ACTIVITY

Learning objectives:

– physical objects are made of a variety of materials

– there are many different objects but fewer types of materials

– the material an object is made of relates to its function

– objects can be grouped according to their properties

1. Sort objects into two sets: **HARD** and **NOT HARD**

   As you do this, enter into the boxes on the worksheet the words (including 'made-up' words) that you use to describe each object.

2. For each word you write, use thesauri, English dictionaries and bilingual dictionaries to find synonyms. Add these synonyms to all boxes on the worksheet as appropriate.

3. Re-sort the objects into **five** sets. Use five of the words you found in thesauri/dictionaries (i.e. alternative terms for HARD and NOT HARD) as names for your five new sets.

4. Now write down a new synonym for each name of each of your five sets. Does it make you want to move any objects?

Follow up the activity by asking each other:

What other physical objects could be added to each set to make the meaning of your set names clearer?

What would you want children to do with the physical objects in order to use some new words meaningfully?

How would you plan for children to use these words in a different context (i.e. without the physical objects) ?

What differences in response will you expect when this is done in children's home language?

according to their texture: smooth, rough, soft etc. On this sort of occasion it is likely that the teacher has targeted a number of concepts and a number of words for the children to understand and operate. Some knowledge of words and word-meanings will be assumed, and some will be deemed to be new, or new in this particular application. A set of objects chosen to fit the categories above may for example invite more evocative lexical units: *spongy, knobbly, furry, sticky, splintery* etc., and provides a rich range of possibilities for negotiation of word meanings with opportunities to draw upon analogies, story lore, onomatopoeia, and L_1-related cultural references.

Negotiating word meaning

What begins to happen when school learning provides EAL pupils with a large range of English vocabulary is that areas of experience become associated with different **semantic domains**. In other words, if you want to talk about your home-related experiences you'll choose L_1 words, and if you have to talk about maths or science or geography, you'll use English words. As long as English grammar is in the stages of being internalised and automated it is likely that L_1 grammar will be used to support the production of English lexemes. This can be observed when children appear to take time to mentally 'rehearse' utterances, inserting English lexemes into incorrect grammatical structures.

Control of L_1 grammatical structure continues to grow for a prolonged period in both speech and writing, and we can expect errors in L_2 for a considerable number of years. In many cases errors cannot be clearly allocated to L_2 development, as the following examples of utterances by English mother-tongue children show:

- There's one which she is nice, and one which she isn't nice (14yr old)
- It's a too hot spoon (5 yr old)
- I'll get a best fork (5 yr old)
- That's the bestest one that I like (7 yr old)

More separation between languages will come with increased automation of English grammar and increased distance between the semantic fields of school and home/community. It is not just a matter of acquiring vocabulary to match L_1 because many of the meanings demanded by school learning simply won't occur at home and therefore the L_1 lexicon will not have developed to cover equivalent semantic fields. What gets important now is not only the process of adding more and more L_2 words, but re-working the meanings of known L_2 words and operating them in a variety of contexts. L_2 takes over in academic domains.

By the time EAL pupils are 7+ they are likely to be using their two (or more) languages in different contexts for different topics and different audiences.

As children add words to their repertoires, they act as if every new word differs in meaning from those already acquired. They rely on the principle

of contrast, that every difference in form marks a difference in
Throughout this early period, they take as their target words that a...
to them – the conventional word-stock of their language community. ... They
adopt the conventional forms they hear and work at assigning to those forms
a plausible meaning. What is plausible is what is consistent with the
apparent meanings being used by adult speakers. Conventionality and contrast apply regardless of language or age: children and adults alike depend
on them for language to work. (Clark, 1993: 241-2)

Clark is here talking about first language acquisition, but her point raises a
number of complex questions about children's conscious awareness of meaning
equivalents across languages when they acquire an additional language sub-
sequent to this early phase of lexical conceptualisation. Where children acquire
two or more words to label real world objects (referents) – book, kitab, libro,
kniga etc. – then clearly they have a conscious awareness that the relationship
between words and their referents is by no means fixed. But when children's use
of L_1 and L_2 vocabulary – particularly in the abstract terms encountered in
curriculum topics – begins to be divided between different semantic domains,
their consciousness of meaning equivalents will be less. A great deal of
cognitive benefit is derived from children discussing the equivalent meanings of
lexical units across languages, and from being taught the L_1 equivalent when the
English term has been learnt first. Adults who are able to use children's home
language and use bilingual dictionaries with them to model this kind of word-
meaning exploration will quickly find that children are eager participants. This
kind of discussion helps to alert EAL learners to such lexical behaviours as
synonymy, wherein word-forms differentiate shades of meanings, and polysemy,
wherein word-forms include more than one meaning. Taking a bilingual
approach to the sorting activity above shows the effects on specific conceptualisation and on the more generic *semantic agility* that children need.

Problems often arise in the use of polysemous items. Young L_2 learners 'fixate'
on a meaning which limits their ability to share the intended meaning of their
teacher or parent. A six year old child was due to go to the dentist for a filling
for the first time and his mother talked to him cheerfully about the funny
buzzing noise that the dentist's drill would make in his mouth. The child, visibly
shocked by the description, burst into tears and his mother could only console
him by saying that she would not take him to the dentist that day.

This (real) anecdote might be taken as a prime case that teachers (and parents!)
need to be alert to children's naïve imaging of such words as *drill*. A successful
learner progressively understands and applies the English word *drill* to a set of
'things' whose common ability to provide a repetitive or sustained rotating
action has the effect of making a hole in the surface upon which it is exerted. A
mental mapping of the set, 'drillhood' is developed, which can include impres-

sions from stored encounters of real world objects or pictures contributing to the set, but is not delineated by them. This allows for the possibility of extension into imagined 'drillhood' and associations which may well be influenced by real world encounters, but may also encompass figurative applications of the word gleaned from story events and an indefinable range of connotations.

The young L_1 speaker was unable to resolve his fear of the dentist's drill because he did not explore the possibility that his reference for the word 'drill' was inappropriate. In this example, fear was probably a major factor inhibiting him from negotiating the meaning of the word, and this and other affective factors are highly significant for many learner inhibitions. We may speculate whether in this instance it is fear or semantic immaturity that is the over-riding inhibitor. The important thing to recognise is that for this child the word *drill* and the images came together in a specific context, and he 'placed' the word in his lexicon accordingly. He couldn't have done it before acquiring at least one image, but for this word he has acquired a particularly vivid collection – images of noise, vibration, power and control, effort/strain, dust/dirt etc. The most relevant factor for the primary teacher in the multilingual classroom, however, is the child's inability to negotiate by a process of retrieval from a set of 'drillhood' which provides enough alternatives to the meaning of the word 'drill' to enable a match between his own images and those of the speaker.

The child's problem was caused by selective and (perhaps due, at least in part, to fear) 'fixated' imaging. His mother was only able to understand his problem when they were out shopping a day or so later and happened to stop and watch a man using a road drill and the child referred *in this context* to his fear of the dentist's drill. In the case of young EAL learners the possibilities of 'fixated' meaning are often precipitated by the pressures of classroom situations, particularly where teachers are not alert to the connotations which may accrue to words. And in interlingual and intercultural communications the weighting of connotations which teacher and child each include in their 'semantic maps' may be particularly problematic. The dentist's drill example shows one child's inability to apply (in this instance) generic characteristics and negotiate a satisfactory addition to his semantic map of a word. The child is unable to reconcile his fixated 'drillhood' with his mother's unconscious use of the word for multiple meanings.

In a retrospective word-association exercise, the mother listed the following:

> *drill*: dentist, high-pitched whine, road-drill, deafening noise, vibration, earache, dirt, rubble, DIY, electric and manual, drill-bit, screws, hole, plaster, army drill, parade, language learning, multiplication tables, fire-drill, drill it into someone, give someone a drilling, shouting, repetitive, rhythmic, propaganda, dull and boring.

The same word association exercise given in English to student-teachers who have acquired English as an additional language produced much smaller combinations of these items. This is not to suggest that a deficiency of associations in L_2 indicates immature semantic map. Other word associations in the students' L_1 are likely to produce comparable lists and, furthermore, enhanced semantic maps when the L_1 and L_2-related connotations are synthesised. Bilingual students have the potential to access and operate richer 'topic meanings' by attending to images from an enlarged cultural repertoire. But instances like this show that 'easy' English words like *drill* may be problematic.

The polysemous nature of *drill* further illustrates that many lexical units express **figurative meaning** as well as literal meaning. Words for which we do not acquire metaphoric meaning remain in low levels of our semantic hierarchy and inhibit our semantic agility. This may be particularly so in L_2 (also in L_1) if words are not used in higher order **abstract** and figurative ways (*squash an argument; squeeze time; press for an answer; push out the boat*).

More abstract ideas involve talking about situations rather than properties. The English word *happy* may be used to express a wide range of abstractions. Other languages will have different ways of differentiating the ideas illustrated below:

HAPPY
which meaning?

happy	→ happy
not happy	→ sad / unhappy
happy because something is good enough	→ satisfied
happy doing something	→ enjoy / like doing something
be willing to do something	→ willing

1. feeling happy

2. feeling extremely happy

3. words for describing someone who is happy most of the time

4. feeling pleased and happy about something that has happened to someone else

5. very happy about something good that has happened

6. happy in an unpleasant way because of something bad that has happened to someone else

7. words for describing an occasion, situation, or period of time when you feel happy

8. a happy feeling

9. to start to feel happy again after feeling sad

10. to make someone feel happy

11. words for describing something such as a story or a piece of music that makes you feel happy

Source: Longman Language Activator (1993)

Inside words

From age two, children begin to attend to internal word structure and this shows itself in new words created to fill gaps in their vocabulary when they need to say something. They begin to attend to **morphemes**, the parts of individual words which affect a word's meaning when changed, as for example, when *walk* becomes *walker* or *walks* or *walking*. Young learners produce, for example, *I goed I wented*, showing that they are discovering the rules of inflection in English. Equivalent errors are made in other languages whose systems of inflection are different and often more complex than English, including, for example, agreements of gender and case markers.

Attention to roots and affixes produce coined adjectival forms -y in *bright/ brighty*; *nice/nicey*; -er -able -ness are added to roots; nouns become agents as in *gun/gunner*; *brush/brusher*, and instruments as in *brakes/braker* and *hider* for an object to hide under (Clark, 1993:118). These features are common in L_2 learners for prolonged stages. A highly fluent Norwegian visitor to York's Viking exhibition protested at the historical inaccuracy of the Vikings' *horny* helmets.

Older learners of EAL and English mother-tongue children also, need to study 'word families' to see how 'free' morphemes (the smallest indivisible grammatical component of a word) and 'bound' morphemes (the components which can't stand on their own) behave in English. **Adverbs** are frequently formed with bound morphemes and are acquired in L_1 later than root nouns or adjectives. This follows the maxim of 'transparency' that is the 'understandability' of root words which children favour:

> Transparency has an outcome of some import for language acquisition: although it is a property of individual words, it encourages the construction of **paradigms** – sets of like forms with related meanings – for example, all agent nouns formed with the suffix -er, all adjectives ending in -y, and so on. Paradigms make up small or large groups of words related in form *and* meaning (Clark, 1993:119)

Young children prefer the simplicity of root forms – nouns before verbs, adjectives before adverbs. In highly inflected languages such as Panjabi or Polish they will stick to the root form of a word and adults will accommodate to this, interpreting their utterances despite their lack of inflections exactly as English-speaking adults interpret English utterances which lack 'function' words (prepositions, pronouns etc.). If this accommodation persists in multilingual classrooms, the danger is that EAL children will persist in use of root forms at the cost of developing transparency of meaning in root + affix forms. After all, if your teacher understands you, you've got your message across.

The morphology of many lexical units extends the meaning potential of their root:

care:	carer	careful	carefully
	careless	carelessly	carefree
	car[e]ing	car[e]ingly	uncaring

Morphology in English is employed in the production of **diminutives.** In L_1 children and adults unconsciously apply bound morphemes: *-y, -ie, -et, -let, -ing* etc. in patterns which are not all so easily acquired in L_2. Some of these amount to 'motherese' as in *doggy, bunny-rabbit*; others fall into sets which trace their etymology; some hold connotations of size or endearment, other appear quite arbitrary:

booklet	bracelet	leaflet	ringlet
duckling	seedling	darling	nestling
chicken	kitten	maiden	bullock
hillock	cigarette	kitchenette	launderette

Like all languages, English endlessly 'coins' new lexical items to express ideas which come into being through cultural dynamics:

- the Chippy

- Twiglets

- Perlette grapes

Words are also divisible into syllables, but **syllabic segmentation** is a phonological division which is different from the semantic segmentation of morphology.[4] Teachers of young children know the importance of children's attunement to syllables when they are learning about how sounds are transformed into writing, and a considerable amount of time is spent on this crucial stage of literacy development in the early years of schooling. Young EAL learners often need extended attention to this aspect of English phonology, as they do to others such as rhyme, onset and rime, alliteration, assonance etc. Older EAL learners who are at early stages of English and many others who show signs of underachievement, will benefit from renewed attention to syllabic segmentation. This needs to be done in ways which suit the children's level of maturation and poetry (including rap), song and jokes provide a host of opportunities for this.

Homophones and polysemous words particularly attract children's attention when they begin to join the 'joke-club' at about age seven. The word-play they enjoy in jokes demonstrates too that they are able to benefit semantically from playing with word boundaries and syllabic segmentation:

SMARTER THAN EIN STEIN.

Your best bet yet

CARLING
Black Label

LAGER
BREWED FOR
A FULL AND
DISTINCTIVE
FLAVOUR

V.ROOMY.

COURIER

The Ford Courier. Van of the Year 1992.

Ford
Everything we do is drive

Knock Knock	Knock Knock	Knock Knock
Who's there?	Who's there?	Who's there?
Who.	Amin.	Olaf.
Who Who?	Amin who?	Olaf who?
Sorry, I don't talk to owls.	I mean me.	Olaf if you think it's so funny.

Children often 'hear' words in non-adult ways:

– I don't like phenomenon in my hair (Prioderm – a lotion for head-lice)

– Where's the jewel carriageway?

Some words which have the same (or nearly the same) sound across languages but quite different meanings can be confusing: Panjabi *ad* (half) and English *add*; whereas others which do have common semantic roots (cognates) can be very helpful, particularly to older EAL learners: Spanish *madre* and English *maternal*; Russian *brat* and English *brother*.

The **onomatopoeic** qualities of language, which children enjoy hugely, are frequent in poetry and EAL learners benefit greatly from word-play which includes attending to these in English and searching for L_1 equivalents:

ONOMATOPOEIA

Alliteration, assonance and rhyme refer to words in relation to each other, starting with the same sound or containing the same vowel sound or ending with the same sound. Onomatopoeia refers to the way an individual word has the power to convey an actual sound and this power is increased when onomatopoeia is combined with alliteration, assonance and rhyme. The following list of onomatopoeic words shows the close relationship with alliteration, words with the same or similar sense tending to begin with the same sound, the s-sounds hissing, the w-sounds whispering, the p-sounds popping and so on.

babble bang blare blast bleat blubber boom bubble buzz bump bark bleep bluster boo bray cackle crackle click clank clink clunk chug crunch croon cluck champ clatter chatter creak cuckoo crash caw chirrup cheep croak coo crow crinkle clang crack chime chuckle drone drip dabble flap flop fizzle fizz frizzle flip gurgle gong gush gabble guzzle growl gobble grunt groan grind giggle grizzle hum hiss hush howl hoot honk hoarse husky jingle jangle lap lash moan murmur miaow mumble munch neigh natter pop patter prattle purr plop puff ping peal pant paddle plug pong pip plonk quack rattle rustle roar rumble ring rasp sizzle splutter swish shuffle snuffle sigh sniff scratch screech squeak scream squeal squelch shriek stutter shrill slap smack snort squawk scrape slam snap twang tinkle tick thud thump twitter tap throb thunder tramp tom-tom whisper whine wheeze whizz wail whinny whack whir whistle yodel yawn yelp yap zoom zip.

Source: *Alliteration, assonance, rhyme and onomatopoeia Pictorial Charts.*

Many meaning units are in the form of **complex words** and **word-compounds**: *birthday, cornflakes, teapot, corkscrew*, and may go unnoticed by native English speakers but might be re-arranged by EAL learners: *Christmas Father; corner street; sunnyshine*. Young L₁ speakers produce *house-smoke* for *chimney smoke*; *car-smoke* for *exhaust* (examples from Clark 1983) and these sorts of compounds in older EAL pupils can substitute for lexical gaps.

– I've got a tummy-ache in my head (4 yr old)

A word may be transferred from one context to another, creating verbs from nouns: *he's keying the door* (Clark 1983); or novel 'blends':

– a doorknob that would not turn was '*stifficult*' (age 5)
– 'I was *smuffercating* when he was sat on me' (age 7).

As adults (teachers and parents) we enjoy these enormously and of course we should enjoy them with EAL pupils, at the same time as noting whether they persist, or whether they have any bearing on comprehension. Word compounds are frequently coined as English needs to incorporate new terms: *keyboard*; *skateboard*; *paragliding*; *stir-fry*. Studying this dimension of language change with children is in itself a way of attending to the lexical gaps of EAL learners. Many compound words lack transparency, and not only for EAL children, for example recent coinages: *interface; screen-dump; hard-copy*. On the other hand, children and adults make up their own compounds for more transparent 'literal' expression of ideas which are opaque in their technical forms: *pain-killer/analgesic; animal doctor/veterinary surgeon.; coughing juice/medicine*.

In larger lexical units non-literal meaning is often hidden by a speaker's (or writer's) use of **euphemism** or **hyperbole** (often occurring in formulaic expressions):

a bit fresh   scorching hot
a bit chilly   a raving lunatic
a spot of bother   a complete shambles

Inevitably the lexical behaviours of euphemism and hyperbole slide into even more opaque metaphoric forms:

- a glutton for punishment

- foaming at the mouth

- on my last legs

Winner (1998) provides a fascinating study of children's understanding of literal and non-literal language, drawing distinctions between metaphor and irony in L_1 locution, and placing non-literal meaning at the centre of children's communicative needs. Meara (1984) found that L_2 learners have more varied and unpredictable patterns of semantic network associations in L_2 than in their L_1 and speculated that learners go through transitional stages in acquisition of L_2 lexicon. Meara, though, was analysing the lexical inferences of older L_2 learners with FL rather than SL learning goals in mind. Though neither L_1 nor FL lexical acquisition provides an explanation of our EAL pupils' experience, each contains important insights upon which teachers are able to draw.

As Ellis (1994) remarks, it is 'premature to speak of anything so defined as an 'order' or a 'sequence' in the L_2 acquisition of lexis' (Ellis 1994:112). A good deal of research remains to be done to 'discover' a developmental pattern of L_2 lexicon, particularly in relation to curriculum learning in UK classrooms and Key Stage needs. In UK classrooms we would expect that L_2 vocabulary development will be highly influenced by context and a hierarchy of needs for curriculum learning. Although time is short in the school-day and teachers have constant pulls on their energies which distract them from the semantic content of classroom activity, it is short-sighted to view vocabulary solely as a means to cover a subject syllabus. It is my belief that attention to the lexical behaviours which underlie L_1 development and can be seen to feature in L_2 in varying levels of proficiency offers a potential framework for targeting vocabulary, aiming not at a narrow, pragmatic collection of 'key words' but at the empowerment of children's innate semantic agility. The next chapter looks in more detail at 'types' of word-meaning and at two approaches to ensure their place in teacher and learner consciousness.

Notes and References

1 A more detailed taxonomy: Strategies For Communication Problems (Lexical Gaps) is provided by Paribakht (1985):

I Linguistic approach

A Semantic contiguity

1 superordinate

2 comparison

a positive comparison

  i analogy

  ii synonymy

b negative comparison

  i contrast and opposition

  ii antonymy

B Circumlocution

1 Physical description

a size

b shape

c colour

d material

2 constituent features

a features

b elaborated features

3 Locational property

4 Historical property

5 Other features

6 Functional description

C Metalinguistic clues

II Contextual approach

A Linguistic context

B Use of target language idioms and proverbs

C Transliteration of L_1 idioms and proverbs

D Idiomatic transfer

III Conceptual approach

A Demonstration

B Exemplification

C Metonymy

IV Mime

A Replacing verbal output

B Accompanying verbal output

Source: Paribakht, T 1985 Applied Linguistics, 6, 132-46 (in Bialystock, 1990).

2 Tough's categories cannot be taken as clear-cut distinctions. There are always problems of definition and overlap in such taxonomies.

3 Thankyou Barré Fitzpatrick for this one!

4 Although they may coincide.

Chapter Three

Words in the classroom

Words change their meanings according to the context in which they occur and EAL pupils must develop the 'semantic agility' – the propensity actively to seek meanings to cope with this. The 'schooling' effects of formal education are well documented (Willes, 1983) and teachers' own observations confirm that children are often either reluctant to indicate or, even worse, unaware of their lack of understanding language and concepts they need so as to progress through the curriculum. As one teacher remarked 'if you have a meaning for it already, why look for another?'[1] If classroom tasks are repeatedly structured in ways which discourage children from semantic enquiry, the result is to dull their appetite for it. Teachers who encourage children to give signals of their non-comprehension and to develop strategies to tackle it, are, conversely, encouraging positive 'meaning-seeking' attitudes.

Nobody would disagree in principle with the need to attend to word-meaning regularly and frequently in multilingual classrooms. But it raises two major causes of concern for teachers: how do we avoid overwhelming EAL learners with language that is too difficult when they are already under-achieving, and how do we find the time for word-meaning exploration in a crowded, content-heavy National Curriculum? This chapter begins by looking at some of the literal/figurative meanings that escape our conscious attention unless we 'deschool' ourselves enough to make fresh encounters with words, as children often have to do. With heightened lexical consciousness we are better equipped to prepare and manage topic discourse in ways which put meaning 'up front'.

Easy Words and Hard Words
Whilst we may be persuaded to think that many aspects of word-meaning are too difficult for EAL learners, children of three delight in using words like *Tyrranosaurus, Diplodocus, Stegosaurus* (see Jan Pieńkowski's *Meg's Eggs*) and they understand their meanings well enough to apply them differentially to dinosaurs with varying characteristics. On the other hand, they have trouble with many little words: *high, low, back, front.*

One child, when asked to count, proceeds to count one to five, on his fingers. When asked, 'Can you count higher?' he raises his hands above his head and again counts one to five on his fingers. When asked, 'Can you count backwards?', he turns round to face the wall and counts again, one to five. Another child is asked to smile for the camera and complies. When asked 'Hold it...' she presses her hands to each side of her mouth (examples from the TV series 'You've Been Framed', Oct 93).

Little 'easy' words are very often **polysemous** and give rise to mis-comprehension, most commonly when they are used to express figurative meanings. These children's interpretations of words support Lakoff and Johnson's (1980) view that metaphoric meaning 'saturates' everyday speech, and that adults are very largely unconscious that this is so when they use L_1. Lakoff and Johnson go so far as to say that all utterances are metaphoric and base much of the argument of their book *Metaphors We Live By* on the behaviour of little words like *high* and *low*. Winner (1988), on the other hand, maintains the distinction between 'literal' and 'non-literal' uses of words for a number of reasons, chief amongst them that figurative expressions *add* meanings which 'literal' expressions lack:

> When Hamlet refers to the world as 'an unweeded garden', 'the metaphoric term (unweeded garden) is actually functioning not as a substitute for the literal term (world) but rather as an *addition*. (Winner, 1988)'.

Metaphors change our perceptions about life and the way we live it. As we take in the range of ideas contained in 'an unweeded garden' our attention is drawn to characteristics of 'world' which we were previously unaware of – that the natural order continually reasserts itself, that order is a balance of power, etc. (Winner, 1988).

Arguments about the nature of metaphor, the distinctions between abstract, figurative, non-literal meanings and literal meanings are to be found in the earliest writings of ancient civilisations, they continue to occupy linguists and philosophers today, not only for purely academic interest, but for the huge potential of language-processing in technological applications. Eileen Cornell Way (1991) grapples with the problems of accommodating figurative meaning in computer programs which process 'natural language'.

> Natural language processing ... requires vast amounts of knowledge; knowledge about the syntax of language, the meaning of words, knowledge about what is assumed as well known in a conversation and what is implied by a particular choice of words.... both literal and metaphoric utterances go beyond the level of the words in the sentences and involve entire semantic domains (Way 1991).

Our world knowledge guides our use of words and our comprehension of words in ways which distinguish our 'cultural intelligence' from 'artificial intelligence':

> ... the amount of common sense background knowledge an average person possesses is enormous: knowledge about what s/he sees, how objects behave in the world, about language, about other people's motives and feelings and more. If we are ever to create a machine that is intelligent we will have to find some way to encode this immense store of knowledge, so that it is accessible in a computer. This is the problem of knowledge representation (Way, 1991).

What we know about the world gives us the power to manipulate words for different effects. In collocation, we have already seen, words acquire multiple meanings and their metaphoric potential may be endlessly extended. The fact that they are so much used in these ways confirms the need for us to teach EAL learners to recognise figurative word behaviour in the relationships of words with one another, and in the way they are contextualised.

In the examples below, *sizzling* and *rabbit* draw their multiple meanings from the way they collocate with other words and with pictures, from the connotations with cultural experience that they elicit, and from the particular intention of the author of the 'text' of each advert. We unconsciously process all these types of

meaning and, if our cultural knowledge provides us with the semantic connections implied in each, we are unconsciously culturally affirmed. Unconscious encounters with metaphor, though, do not give us the power to manipulate polysemous words in the way that conscious attention to them does. The more connections like this that EAL learners are alert to, the better equipped they are to control polysemous words for their own meanings. The child who understands the abstraction of, for example, *build, building*, instead of being limited to the idea of 'a building' being only a physical entity such as a house or a school, is able to construct original metaphors which further extend her perceptions about life, relationships, human emotion and more (see opposite).

It would be illuminating to match Yasmin's use of 'build' metaphors in English with equivalents in other languages.

Metaphor, idiom, cliché

Metaphors are necessary to the cohesion of cultural groups and command of metaphoric expression in English is a vital means for EAL learners to a shared national culture which depends on the English language for cohesion. This does not imply that L_1 metaphors are less important: on the contrary, the confident cultural grounding that all children need in their home life will not be served by bland transactional expressions – 'give me the salt' and such-like. Children need to encounter and manipulate L_1 metaphoric meanings in ways which maintain

Building a poem

My teacher told me this morning
that can you build
So I looked up books
And I found amazing words
 Which made me jump in the air
I found things like
I can build a wall
In my garden
 strong big and tall
 I can build a wall inside me
If I am upset with somebody
I can build a wall between me and you
 But I don't want to
 you know what I mean
I can build words inside me
 And make a story
to share with you.
I look out of my window
 And I see traffic building up
 In my street.
And I am cross
 And anger builds up inside me.
 Now you see
 you can build lot of words
 with me.

By yasmin

age 9

Yasmin, Manningham Middle School, 1996

the bonds between generations, between country of heritage and country of settlement, between home and school.

Richards (1936) saw metaphor as 'the omnipresent principle of language', declaring that 'we cannot get through three sentences of ordinary, fluid discourse without it.' For young EAL learners, and for children in L$_1$, even 'dead' metaphors (that is ones which have become so clichéd that fluent adults hardly think of them as metaphors) are novel:

running water
foot of the mountain
leaf of a book
I can't swallow that
half-baked ideas

I can't take my eyes off her.
He hasn't got an honest bone in his body.
(examples from Lakoff and Johnson (1980)

Fluent speakers of a language persistently ignore the 'literal truth' value of many things they say:

My common sense literally flew out of the window.
John was literally glued to the television set.
(examples from Way, 1991)

Literal truth frequently goes out of the window in the many idioms which every language makes its own. When learning English, as with other languages, we have to appreciate that idioms operate as lexical units – many of them with metaphorical meanings that puzzle EAL learners:

'Wordsworth was a poet who answered the call of nature' (exam answer)

Idioms are the cultural keys to a language. With command of idiom, additional language learners are able to harness the energy of the language they are acquiring and contribute their own inter-cultural metaphors in powerful ways. Just as EAL learners need to penetrate the figurative meanings of English idioms, so do they also need to absorb the equivalent range of figurative expression in L$_1$.

swings and roundabouts	hold your horses
between the devil and the deep blue sea	look before you leap
at the end of the day	you can't run before you can walk
going round the houses	at the drop of a hat
beating about the bush	in the heat of the moment
making a meal of it	in the wink of an eye

bite the bullet	come what may
grasp the nettle	come hell or high water
face the music	in for a penny, in for a pound

Idioms are drawn from **storylore**: sleeping beauty; dog in a manger; the goose that lays the golden eggs; pay the piper; and from **parables:** feeding of the five thousand; at the eleventh hour. They have the force of folk wisdom in **proverbs**: in for a penny, in for a pound; don't count your chickens before they're hatched. They mask **hyperbole**: on my last legs; complete and utter rubbish; I could eat a horse. They mask **euphemism**: a bit of a lad; not much fun; pass away. When we are asking EAL children to gradually acquire a repertoire of such idioms, we can affirm their cultural allegiance to their home language by matching English idioms with L_1. English mother-tongue children also benefit from hearing the 'literal' translation of equivalent idioms from different languages, since this frequently highlights the metaphoric meaning of the phrases they use as unanalysed chunks.

But in addition to their emotional and social import, metaphoric expressions activate semantic processes which affect children's thinking:

> A novel metaphor surprises the listener and challenges him/her to solve a puzzle by mapping attributes and relations between the stated or implied elements being linked (Gentner, 1983). Literal descriptions do no such thing but simply describe the world in established ways. In the sense that metaphors force us to understand one thing in terms of another, metaphors must elicit cognitive processes not ordinarily called upon by literal language (MacCormac, 1985 in Winner, 1988).

Lakoff and Johnson (1980) make a similar point:

> ...The purpose of metaphor is not precision, but rather to bring out higher levels or *more abstract* connections between concepts, ones which might not ordinarily be noticed (1980).

This purpose, of course, is central to what we think of as 'poetic' language. But more than that, it is central to our communication of many ideas:

> ...it is easier to take parts from other established concepts than to build up new ones from scratch. The use of metaphor to extend our concepts in science is legendary: the Bohr model of the atom uses the structure of the solar system; Maxwell's represents an electrical field in terms of the properties of a fluid, atoms as billiard balls etc. Thus even science is not the paradigm of literal language it was once considered to be; rather, metaphor is vital to the modelling processes that result in advances of science (Way, 1991).

The use of metaphors in science does not define ideas in any precise sense, but attempts to explain abstractions. This often works well for learners who have a sound grasp of the intended 'imaging' contained in the metaphor, but will only work if the connection between ideas (for example, between atoms and billiard balls) coincides with the learners' cultural experiences. We are to some extent aware of how some kinds of metaphors drawn from gender-related occupations (aspects of sport or fashion, for example) are sometimes understood by boys but not by girls, and vice versa. For EAL learners it is often more effective to draw on **analogies** with home and community experiences, and teachers who can do this in children's home language have a great advantage here. Analogy is an explicit way of connecting a new idea to a familiar one: 'it's like when you...' ; 'you know when you...' ; 'think what it's like when you...' etc. These sorts of **cultural connotations** help children to 'situate' abstractions – but they need checking! Ask children to talk about the images they are drawing on from their own experiences to avoid their going off on a tangent of their own and losing the thread of the meanings they need to attend to in the classroom.

Finding the home language equivalent can be difficult when so many apparently easy English words are polysemous – used for literal, abstract, figurative meanings.'The fact is, *there are no context-free meanings* for either literal or metaphoric utterances' (Way, 1991). Children must recognise the need to apply word-meanings differently in subject areas, e.g. for *line* there are geography meanings, history meanings, maths meanings, PE meanings etc., and dozens more ways of using the word figuratively, e.g. *snowline, treeline, line of descent, line up, parallel line, make a bee-line; toe the line, line of argument, the bottom line, deadline, line your pockets...*

We continue to learn this throughout life as we weave in and out of different semantic fields. In a (somewhat untypical) week I dealt with an electrician, a chimney sweep, a solicitor, a funeral director, a landlord, a double-glazing firm and a computer technician, not to mention the usual run of educational colleagues. With the electrician I discussed *points* and *earths, positive and negative charges,* and how to *trip a fuse*; from the chimney sweep I learned how *a clean flue draws fire*, and cement *goes off*; the solicitor talked about *titles* and *deeds*; my young niece wanted to know why we weren't wearing *mourning dresses* at the funeral; the landlord wanted a *bond*; the *glazing* technician pressed me to make decisions about *extrusions* and *architraves*, and the *software consultant* enthused about *extensions, archives* and *environments*. Some of these lexical items may appear to express quite specific 'concrete' objects – the meaning of architrave, for example, is easy enough to learn when you are able to see the actual object, or a picture of it. But is it? When you look at an architrave you have to appreciate that it is the *organisation* of wood or plaster (or in this case, plastic) which makes the idea of an architrave 'real'. The Shorter

Oxford Dictionary defines an architrave as a 'collective name for the parts (lintel, jambs and their mouldings) that surround a doorway or window'. The very same pieces of wood, when organised differently, would be labelled as 'skirting', or 'casing'.

The word *architrave* is therefore the expression of an idea about organising bits of wood or plastic. I also had to learn that *archives* and *environments* are, similarly, ideas for organising digits on the computer. It is easy to see that these and many other words used in 'computerspeak' are borrowed from older fields of architecture and libraries, and this gives us some (small) understanding of what is going on inside the computer. To make sense of the words though, I have to loosen my attachment to mental images of shelves in the library, and buildings in the street, and construct a mental **abstraction** for *archive* and *environment*. It is the abstract idea of *archive* which provides the connection between library shelves and electronic files, and it is the abstract idea of *environment* which connects city streets and digitised information. These abstract connections underpin academic learning.

You may be thinking that all this is too complex to apply to children's classroom learning. Not so. The classroom provides some very apt devices for developing children's understanding of abstract ideas contained in words. Wall displays (Services, page 83) can be used to teach children the abstract connections which allow us to use a word in varying contexts:

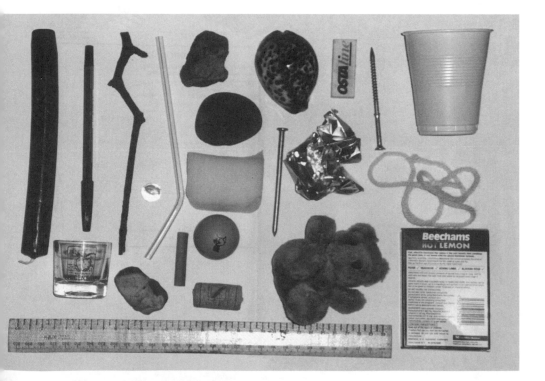

In the sorts of discussions which these displays evoke, opportunities arise for children to make connections between home life and academic ideas and they will do a lot of this connecting more efficiently by using L₁ as well as English. For young children the collection of sorting objects I used earlier (See page 63 and opposite) can be used to pose questions: when does a stick become a twig or a ruler?; when does a stone become a pebble?; when do we call a piece of foam a 'sponge'?

Leech (1974) made a distinction between 'conceptual meaning' and 'associative meaning', and further refined his distinction as 'seven types of meaning':

1. CONCEPTUAL MEANING or Sense		Logical, cognitive, or denotative content.
	2. CONNOTATIVE MEANING	What is communicated by virtue of what language refers to ['over and above its purely conceptual content'].
	3. SOCIAL MEANING	What is communicated of the social circumstances of language use.
ASSOCIATIVE MEANING	4. AFFECTIVE MEANING	What is communicated of the feelings and attitudes of the speaker/writer.
	5. REFLECTED MEANING	What is communicated through association with another sense of the same expression.
	6. COLLOCATIVE MEANING	What is communicated through association with words which tend to occur in the environment of another word.
	7. THEMATIC MEANING	What is communicated by the way in which the message is organised in terms of order and emphasis.

Leech, G. (1974)

The main distinction here is between conceptual meaning and associative meaning. In theoretical semantics it is the *denotative* content which gives words their logical 'value'. But young children, and most adults, are not logicians. The 'value' we place on words has more to do with their communicative effect than with any strict rule of semantic theory. EAL pupils need to develop an attitude to word meaning which leads them to seek for meaning in all the aspects Leech identifies. I would even say that it is the types of associative meaning which need most attention from teachers and learners. If we try to limit classroom language to the 'easy' words, we deny EAL children the rich expression that makes a language worth learning and worth using to share experiences and ideas:

> the danger is that children are denied engagement with the technical terms, the rich range of figurative and polysemous lexical units, the cultural

analogies, and the 'chained' textual metaphors that characterise academic rhetoric, and much written text. We believe that this damage is (wholly unintentionally) pernicious. (Fitzpatrick and McWilliam, 1995)

Attempts to keep 'difficult' words out of teacher-talk are anyway doomed to failure. Conteh *et al* (1995) report on a study of the teacher language used to present and explore primary curriculum topics:

> In total we found ninety nine instances of metaphorical uses of language (logged over seven episodes of about 25/30 minutes)... The picture painted by these data is of a metaphorically image-rich discourse where the language has encoded abstractions and propositions in largely perceptual terms to aid our understanding and manipulation of complex ideas and phenomena. (Conteh *et al.*,1995)

The findings of this study concur with the thinking of Lakoff and Johnson (1980): it is impossible, even when we try to 'simplify' teacher-talk for EAL pupils, to avoid figurative expression. Talk or written text can be heavily loaded with metaphoric meaning and children's attention to the forms and relationships of these lexical units has limited capacity:

> ... many of the metaphorical uses of language embedded in the teacher's normal discourse are likely to be ignored unless they are frequent or highly salient to the conduct of the classroom. Where it is important for the child to understand the meanings which the teacher uses, e.g. where a verbal response is required, the child has the task of threading her way through a dense and complex pattern of literal and metaphoric meanings with many opportunities for misunderstanding. (Fitzpatrick and McWilliam 1995).

Fitzpatrick (1996) summarises the need to attend consciously to figurative language in the multilingual classroom:

- it is what we take for granted
- it is often the key to understanding
- it is often the trigger for misunderstanding
- we cannot avoid figurative language so we have to 'manage' the meaning
- anticipate multi-meanings of words which are key words in the topic or in the way in which you intend to talk about the topic
- use analogies or extended metaphors which relate to children's experience
- when multi-meaning words occur, explore them in a wide variety of senses but particularly those which make semantic connections with the focal new meaning

–   use the children's understandings of possible meanings as the baseline wherever you can

–   create a classroom 'consciously curious' about meanings of words.

(*source*: Fitzpatrick, 1996)

What we need then are approaches to managing the curriculum which apply our insights into figurative or abstract word-meanings to a fresh empathy with EAL learners' need for engagement with those meanings.

Rich Scripting

No classroom scenario is fully predictable, but we can anticipate or orchestrate some balance of planned and spontaneous discourse based on the activity or subject area. For younger EAL learners the need for repetitive exposure to, and operation of, new vocabulary is generally appreciated by teachers; with older EAL learners, the pressure of subject syllabi often demands that comprehension be a good deal more rapid. With a content-heavy curriculum we may over-rely on teacher-talk and written texts for its 'delivery', rather than on activities or visual aids which encourage meaning-seeking. It is of course impossible to stop and check comprehension of every word that EAL pupils encounter, but if our assumptions about shared linguistic and cultural frameworks go unexamined, we contribute to, rather than alleviate EAL learners' difficulties. Taking a 'Rich Scripting' approach to activity and lesson planning means identifying the key lexical items (words and phrases) necessary to the concepts and skills which are the expected outcomes of the activity or lesson.

To begin with, this 'Rich Scripting' idea is similar to identifying 'Keywords' for topics/subjects – an approach many teachers already use to get children to pay attention to 'technical' terminology in, for example, geography or mathematics. It is also, initially, similar to the use of glossaries in textbooks where the keywords of a topic are explained in the form of a simple dictionary. This too is a device that many schools extend to the use of word-books or, for older pupils, personal logbooks. Glossaries though, are based on the idea of *defining* words in a particular 'sense' and their usefulness lies in how clearly they delineate the meanings of words for specific contexts. For example, a glossary in a topic book on cereals may include *grain* and will define it as 'a single seed' or 'small, hard and roundish seed from a cereal plant'. It will not include other possible meanings of *grain*.

Ashton-Warner (1963) made much of 'Key Words' in teaching Maori children to read. Her approach was based on a strong conviction that 'first words must have an intense meaning' if children are to internalise a personal relevance in reading. The 'cultural' meanings of words must draw children rather than confound and distance them. Eve Gregory (1996) builds this powerful idea into her 'lexical knowledge centre' – one of the sets of 'clues' that children use in reading for meaning in an additional language.

Rich Scripting, however, takes the idea of Keywords or '**target lexical items**' as I prefer to call them, and applies to them a framework of lexical behaviours – it goes beyond giving learners the *definitions* of words to getting them to examine the *meaning potential* of words. Rich Scripting is a way of planning processes of engagement with word meaning in topic/subject areas and also helps children to see how words and phrases change their meanings according to how they are used.

The two dimensions of planning and implementation in the Rich Scripting of target lexical items pose three key questions:

Planning

– **demands**: certain word-meanings will be required for the focus of the activity/lesson and these will be closely matched to the expected learning objectives, i.e. the concepts and/or skills. So the activity/lesson will demand understanding of target lexical items used in particular ways.

Q. Which lexical items (words and phrases) do the pupils have to understand and use if they are to participate successfully in the learning?

– **opportunities**: the activity/lesson will provide opportunities for the target lexical items to be used in ways which extend *beyond* the immediate learning objectives. This means that the teacher will plan to use the target lexical items in ways which alert children to its particular meaning in the activity/lesson *and* its wider meaning potential.

Q. How can attention to lexical items in this activity/lesson extend the English lexicon of the pupils generally?

Implementation

– **strategies**: the management of attention to word-meaning by teacher and learners. The teacher will model the 'meaning-seeking' attitude that we want learners to adopt. The activity/lesson will be structured to encourage 'shared imaging', use of appropriate resources (e.g. dictionaries, OHP and blackboard) and L_1.

Q. Which teaching techniques clearly focus attention on lexical forms and meanings, and nurture the semantic agility of learners?

The Rich Scripting sheet opposite gives an example of planning for a geography (Key Stage 2) lesson. A blank sheet is provided on page 90.

Rich Scripting: demands, opportunities and strategies

date............... group/class...5T............ subject/topic...Mountains (Mt. Blanc).....................................

Target Lexical Items (words and phrases)

Peak

mountain peak

Meaning-seeking: strategies

- model own use of thesaurus, dictionaries (incl. bilingual)
- time for paired consultation in home languages
- time for paired use of dictionaries
- use blackboard to collect meanings, including L_1 equivalents
- use OHP to show own/pupils' research, for text highlighting etc
- shared imaging
- words and phrases for home research
- displays/data-bases/glossaries and word-books
- spotlight activities/free choice time
- cross-curricular collaboration

Categories for exploring meaning potential	ENGLISH	OTHER LANGUAGES
• English synonyms (or near) and L_1 equivalents	top, summit walks in the Peak District	pic sommet Gipfel höhepunkt pico
• analogies (incl. personal associations)		
• multiple meanings (literal, figurative, connotative)	peak of singer's career peak of my baseball cap	(i.e langs. around Mt. Blanc
• homonyms (or near, and incl. jokes, play on words and rhymes)	take a quick peek/play peek-a-boo! fit of pique, feeling peaky	
• collocations incl. phrasal verbs, compounds, coordinates	peak-hour traffic	
• idiomatic phrases and 'chunks' (incl. proverbs, homilies, clichés)	I'm past my peak I don't want to peak too early!	
• differentiated meanings ('it's not the same as...')	pick, perk, pecan nuts peacock, Pekinese dog	
• word families/related words (incl. superordinates, antonyms)	base, foot, bottom	
• root and affixes (incl. n., vb., adj., adv.)		
• etymology (origin and history)	beak (Irish)	

Rich Scripting: demands, opportunities and strategies

date............... group/class............... subject/topic..

Target Lexical Items (words and phrases)	Meaning-seeking: strategies
	• model own use of thesaurus, dictionaries (incl. bilingual)
	• time for paired consultation in home languages
	• time for paired use of dictionaries
	• use blackboard to collect meanings, including L_1 equivalents
	• use OHP to show own/pupils' research, for text highlighting etc
	• shared imaging
	• words and phrases for home research
	• displays/data-bases/glossaries and word-books
	• spotlight activities/free choice time
	• cross-curricular collaboration

Categories for exploring meaning potential	ENGLISH	OTHER LANGUAGES
• English synonyms (or near) and L_1 equivalents		
• analogies (incl. personal associations)		
• multiple meanings (literal, figurative, connotative)		
• homonyms (or near, and incl. jokes, play on words and rhymes)		
• collocations incl. phrasal verbs, compounds, coordinates		
• idiomatic phrases and 'chunks' (incl. proverbs, homilies, clichés)		
• differentiated meanings ('it's not the same as...')		
• word families/related words (incl. superordinates, antonyms)		
• root and affixes (incl. n., vb., adj., adv.)		
• etymology (origin and history)		

Using this Rich Scripting sheet as part of lesson preparation affects the lexical consciousness of the teacher by drawing attention to three important processes:

* consciousness of the meaning potential of words;

* consciousness of children's possible interpretations of words;

* consciousness of cultural frameworks in using and understanding words.

I am not proposing that every lesson plan should involve filling out a Rich Scripting sheet as fully as the one shown above! The list of lexical behaviours that serve as prompts against which to check the meaning potential of the target lexical items for the activity/lesson are not all applicable in every case and for every learning situation. Neither are they always neatly distinct from each other, and it is unnecessarily time-consuming for example, trying to decide whether a word belongs in the category of collocations or of multiple meanings, since very often words acquire metaphoric meaning in collocation. Similarly, we can get into too many technicalities about whether or not a word with multiple meanings is a true homonym. What matters is how the Rich Scripting sheet helps us see the **meaning potential** of words and phrases we will want EAL learners to understand and use in relation to the ideas they will be focusing on.

Take, for example as target lexical items, *snowline* and *treeline* – both compound words which use *line* for specific technical meanings in the geography topic of mountains. The word line is one of those 'easy' words which escape our notice until we ask the question: 'What does *line* mean? 'One answer may be, 'It depends. What sort of line do you mean?' Geography teachers are very aware of the difficulty posed by understanding *snowline* and *treeline*. The two uses of *line* ask for opposing abstractions: a snowline is the land height to which snow reaches *down*, whereas a treeline is the land height *up* to which trees grow[2]. But knowing these specific technical meanings of *line* can cause us to block awareness of a word's potential other meanings. Neat definitions for *snowline* and *treeline* may also prevent us from attending to the core concept of *line* and prevent children from doing so as well. They may well acquire the words, use the words in expected ways, but not grasp the meanings.

One teacher[2] began a Year 5 geography lesson by distributing a collection of cards to pairs of children intending to alert them meanings in word compounds and multisyllabic words:

scenery	portrait	telescope
landscape	snowline	view
seascape	line-up	microscope
treeline	skyline	beeline

After giving them time to discuss their ideas about the meanings of the words, he asked them to group the words in sets. The *line* words then became the focus of a class discussion. Reading from entry line in the **Longman Contemporary Dictionary of English**, the teacher asked the children to decide which of the phrases that he found in the dictionary might belong in the geography lesson and why. I have added more collocations for the headword LINE:

clothes-line	telephone line	hemline
dotted line	line up	outline
fine line	stateline	railway line
fishing line	on the right lines	line of argument
line your pockets	line your nest	line of fire

The teacher was trying to get the children to realise that the little word *line* has the potential to mean many different things, that a 'line' is an **idea** as well as a thing that you can draw or measure. He intended the children to become aware that they would need to look for yet more meanings of *line* when they came to look at the meaning of *snowline* and *treeline* in the context of mountains.

T Ooh what a strange group of words. *Underline, skyline, treeline, snow line*, What else have we got?

pp (Pupils) *snowline skyline line up*

T Yeh, strange group of words. Does anybody know what any of those words mean? I'll try Imran.

Im Do they go in a line?

T They don't all mean the same thing. They're all different. Some of them are nearly the same, but they're all different.

Imran shows that he sees the common element *line* in the words, and his question might also indicate that he thinks (at least in this instance) of a 'line' as 'a long, thin arrangement of things'. If invited to elaborate he might have been able to give his teacher a clearer idea of his mental construct of 'line'.

pp ......

T a line of trees. *Treeline.* You think *treeline* is a line of trees. Well you're nearly right, [p...] a line of trees, I've got that one written down. I was just going to ask you if a treeline was a line of trees. It isn't, not quite, not quite. So a *treeline* is not really a line of trees.

The teacher has anticipated the children's idea of 'a line of trees'. Again the pupil appears to have a 'long, thin arrangement' idea of 'line' and (much easier to see this when we have the transcript to examine!) his teacher might have compared his idea to Imran's so that they, and others in the class could see the abstract idea of 'line' that the two boys have.

T Are there any others? Do you know what *line up* means?

boy Yeh, when people make a straight line

T When people have to get into a line. What are they doing? they're forming a –

boy ... they make a line ... when there's a fire....

T That's right, yes, they're making a line, making a line....if there's a fire bell or a fire alarm or something like that they might be making a line to go outside. What do we call it though when people line up at a bus stop or outside a shop, or outside the school shop, or line up to get an injection. [p....] Ooh, what do we call it, forming a, we're making a what?

p Queue

T Queue, right, good. We're making a queue, well done P. So if you're lining up you're making a queue. So we do know what one of those words means, don't we X, what's *line up* mean?

p ....

T ... Go on say it again.

p ....When people...

T When people line up and they make a line or a queue, right. ...

Another example of the 'long, thin arrangement' idea of 'line' which the teacher is now re-enforcing. The class enjoy a collective frisson at the mention of injections, but they are not invited to contribute own their images of *line up*. This is a pity because the 'long, thin arrangement' idea of 'line' is now modified by the 'waiting in turn for something' idea of the proposed synonym *queue* (which means it is not a pure synonym).

T What does that one mean then? *underline*. Come on Rizwaan, what does *underline* mean? It's got the word *line* in it. Does it mean make a line under something?

pp no/yeh.....

T What with? a line of people? under the table?

pp No.../...like make a line under a word

T Make a line under a word. With what?

p ..../...

T   With a ruler. What do you draw it with? what do make the line with?

p   Pencil

T   Pencil or a pen, yes. So that word's got *line* in it, but it's a different word. *line up, underline.* ... different. eh?. <u>up</u> and <u>under</u>. They're almost opposites. Almost opposites.

Are they 'opposites' though? I don't think the teacher was sure himself. He might have asked the children what they thought, but is probably wiser to leave this idea aside for now, or, better, note it for a teacher to attend to in an English lesson. Another common factor in the idea of 'line' emerges here – the 'straightness' idea that comes with using a ruler to underline, and also implied is the idea of 'fine mark' in a line drawn by pencil. *Underline* and *line up* express actions (they are verbs) rather than states or entities, so 'underlining' with a pencil amounts to making a long thin mark. This is not the meaning the teacher wants the children to apply to *snowline* and *treeline*. He needs to point out this difference.

T   Who's got that one, *skyline*. Does anyone know what *skyline* means. Do you think it's a line in the sky?

pp   no........

T   Could it be line in the sky?

pp   yes...

T   No it's not. *skyline, skyline* [p...] is the line that the land makes against the –

pp   sky

T   sky. look, [shows photo] as far as you can see in the landscape –

girl   ....rocket...

T   A rocket could make a line in the sky, couldn't it. [p...] It could, yes, or an aeroplane could make a line in the sky, [p...] but that's not called a *skyline.* Look, a *skyline* is as far as you can see on a landscape. So if you are looking at a view or a landscape, the furthest bit of land that you can see is the *skyline.* We can't see very far today, but looking out of that window there, what can you see against the *skyline*? What can you see the top of against the *skyline*? or the shape of?

p   ...chimneys

T   The chimneys, yes. What else? Anything else?

pp   .... house ....

T   The houses, the tops of the houses, yes.

p   ...fog...

T   You can see the fog, yes, but we're not thinking – the fog isn't the skyline. What can we see against the fog?

pp   house.../ the church

T   The church, the chimneys, the roofs, the aerials, the tops of the houses, the tops of the buildings. [p...] That's the *skyline*. I wonder if we're any closer to understanding what *snowline* means [p...] *snowline*. Could it be, could it be, a line in the snow?

pp   no/no

T   I don't think so either. It's quite a difficult one to understand...but look at this picture here [p...]

The rather abrupt jump from *skyline* to *snowline* here is probably due to the teacher's anxiety about using up all the geography lesson with this attention to words. It is a 'meeting along a length of border' idea of 'line' that is contained in *skyline* (i.e. meeting of sky and land), and this is the meaning he wants children to apply to *snowline* (meeting of land covered in snow and land without snow).

A colleague reading the transcript observed that the teacher would have better served the 'geography' meaning of *line* in *snowline* if his Rich Scripting had drawn out the 'essential concept' of a 'line' in each of the words. The *definition* of *skyline* he provides – '*skyline* is as far as you can see on a landscape' – is not untrue, but it doesn't attend to one of the essential idea of 'line' as 'meeting along a length of border'.

The teacher's questions elicit the idea of a rocket making a line in the sky, and, since the lesson took place in November, this is very likely to come from associations with fireworks for Plot Night or Diwali, providing a good opportunity to draw a contrast of meaning by referring to the children's experiences.

If the teacher's Rich Scripting planning of *snowline* and *treeline* had identified the different abstractions in the 'line' words – the 'going somewhere' idea, the 'straight and thin' idea and the 'meeting along a length of border' idea – he might have anticipated ways of using the children's ideas to highlight these. The blackboard is asking to be used for graphic illustrations of these different abstractions. He could also have asked the children to act out the three abstractions.

In the next extract, two unplanned uses of *line* and *point* occur and could be confusing for EAL learners. In between them the teacher says 'and it doesn't have to be straight line, does it?' – an essential part of understanding *snowline* and *treeline* which gets hidden in his anxiety to provide a definition.

[Interval. Pupils are looking at different photos and the teacher has explained *snowline*]

Right then what do you think this one is?

p   …

T   A *treeline*. we've already said it's not the same as a line of trees. If the snowline is the line at which the snow comes down to, [p…] what do you think the *treeline* might be?

p   ….

p   trees die

T   Where the leaves are at the top. Not quite. You're on the right lines. When trees die…

p   where the snow comes

T   No, not where the snow comes.

p   Where the trees come down

T   Where the trees grow to. So lower down the mountain we have lots of trees. But as it gets colder the trees won't grow. So we reach a point, or a line and it doesn't have to be straight line, does it, but we reach a point where we can say that is a *treeline* [p…] because the trees won't grow any higher up the mountain than that, because it is too-

pp   cold

T   cold, or the soil is too thin. So when we talk about the *snowline* we're talking about the line where the snow comes <u>down</u> to, because it's too warm and the snow doesn't come down any further than that. When we're talking about the *treeline* we're talking about the line where the trees go <u>up</u> to, because they won't grow any higher than that because it's too cold.

The children now have definitions for *snowline* and *treeline*. We don't know whether they have grasped the essential difference between the possible meanings of line – as a visible mark (made by a pencil or a rocket), as an arrangement of things (people, trees etc.) and as meeting along a length of border. They've certainly realised that they're meant to be thinking about words with line in them. The next extract introduces a nice touch of humour and a memorable image of beeline. I feel it leaves the understanding of *snowline* and *treeline* incomplete since the essential 'straightness' idea of 'line' in *beeline* is very different from the essential 'meeting along a length of border' of *snowline* and *treeline* which, more often that not, are not straight. Note also the polysemous uses of *make* and *like* ...

T   Have we got one [card] that we haven't talked about?

p   *beeline*

T   *beeline* – what does that mean? *beeline*

p   Sir, the line of a bee [pupils laugh]

T   line of a bee. Not quite [pp....] not quite. If you make a *beeline* for something, you're doing something

p   you're making a bee

T   you're not making a bee, no. [p...] Making a *beeline* for something means that you're going straight to something [pp...], so a *beeline* is a –

pp straight line

T   a straight line. So if somebody came in here and made a *beeline* straight for Christopher. They'd come in and they'd go straight across the room, like a bee who's come in the room and goes, Ha! a flower, bzzzzzzz zzzzzzzzzzz [pp laugh] yes? A *beeline* is a straight line. And it's a saying, if you make a *beeline* for something, it's like saying you go straight to it, straight away. If your mum's laid out lots of food and your favourite food is in the middle and you go straight to your favourite food, you make a –

p   *beeline*

T   *beeline*, straight to it.

p   ... bees like flowers

T   Like a bee goes to a flower. Yes. Right. Now then, [shows word card] this is the one we're interested in today [pp...] *Snowline*. What I'd like you to do tonight, is take this home with you and try and.............

[gives instructions for finding out L₁ equivalents as homework] ...

Demands and opportunities

The Rich Scripting idea is intended to identify the lexical **demands** of a topic, i.e. the meanings which are at the centre of the learning. The lexical demands in this case are the 'geography' definitions for *snowline* and *treeline*, and although the teacher did eventually give these to the children, it seems to me that this would have been a lot more useful to them earlier on, so that the teacher would have had frequent cause to remind them of the 'geography' ideas in the two terms by exploring other differentiated meanings of *line*. Rich Scripting is not intended to withhold meanings that are important in the hope that children will come to discover them in a roundabout way, even though there may be much to learn by doing this. With so much to cover in National Curriculum topics I think it is a much more effective use of time to provide a clearly contextualised target meaning (in this case with pictures and/or three-dimensional models) and to reinforce this meaning by comparing/contrasting it with other possible meanings. *Snowline* and *treeline* therefore remain the point of reference for all the other possible meanings of *line*. What this alerts children to is that definitions are not simply formulas that they have to repeat but ideas that they must connect and contrast with other ideas.

It is easy to criticise on the basis of a transcript, and I greatly admire the teacher's willingness to make the recording and to allow criticism to be made by colleagues. The geography teacher himself was anxious about the amount of time spent on the words, worrying that this was done at the expense of attending to the geography. This is an anxiety which, without doubt, has been increased since National Curriculum programmes of study have forced the pace of curriculum delivery. With the pressures of a content-heavy National Curriculum EAL children are at even greater risk of a conforming to a 'tasks for ticks' syndrome, especially in classrooms which lack opportunities for children to ask questions about words, discuss words in the texts they read, and explore word-meaning in varied, purposeful ways. The dilemma is not about choosing to spend time teaching language or time teaching geography, it is about having enough time to teach the subject ideas effectively. If children don't understand the meanings of words like *snowline* and *treeline*, then they don't understand the geography concepts. The words are the geography.

The approach was tried by other teachers taking the same Year Five class. In a history lesson with work on family trees, *line* featured as *line of descent* and *time-line*. The children's willingness to pay attention to the meanings of the words was obvious and they were able to make clear connections with the 'line' meanings they had discussed in the geography lesson. Although the geography teacher felt dissatisfied with the way he had handled the lesson, he had certainly made a difference to the children's lexical consciousness. An English lesson[3] provided further opportunities to pay attention to some of the other words arising in the geography topic. One child lay on a table and the teacher described her face as a 'landscape'. The children picked up the idea and extended it – her eyes were pools, her nose was a mountain peak, her mouth was a cave. Thus, words carried from one context to another are seen by EAL learners to represent different meanings which they must consciously attend to.

One of the laudable intentions of NC Programmes of Study has been to promote coherence of subject content between age-phases. In principle, this means that a whole-school approach will ensure that progression of content is built on pupils' incremental understanding and knowledge. In practical management terms it comes down to the distribution of topics into yearly programmes which 'cover' the content prescribed and tested at each Key Stage. For EAL pupils and for many English mother-tongue pupils the net effect may be a fragmentary series of activities which prevent genuine engagement with the ideas contained in words. Children become habituated to *doing* rather than *understanding*.

The focal learning objectives of each curriculum activity make demands on children's lexicon and each activity additionally provides opportunities to extend lexical knowledge more widely. How the balance of demands and opportunities for different activities is managed will depends on teachers' judgements about each child's knowledge base and what kind of extension is appropriate. All children need frequent opportunities to explore word meanings in ways which develop their conscious attention to how words work and cultivate their curiosity about words. EAL learners need to do this more frequently and also need time to review, with a teacher's help, lexical items which they have encountered and wish to explore. This has many implications for group-work.

The history teacher[4] provides a transcript of a group discussion about parish workhouses with the same Year 5 class. The teacher leads on from *workhouse* to other *compound words* which include *work,* such as *housework* and *homework*, and they play around with *work* and *house* to find combinations with other words. The idea of 'donkeywork' is introduced:

boy Work a donkey in a donkey house...

'I' donkey house!

p fixing work

T fixing work. What about *donkey* work?

J plumber work

T Oh you've learnt about plumbing work haven't you, what's a plumber, Javed?

J He....... he fix the pipes

T oh he doesn't mend plums any more

J [laughs] no

T [laughs] N said *donkey work*, I know what she means..

boy donkeys carry stuff.. carry on their back, miss, and camels boy ....picture.......

T   I hear people say donkey work I've never heard people say *camel work*, but they both do the same thing

boy horse work

T   If I said, Oh, making this bonfire is real donkey work, would I be using a donkey?

pp   no....... wood

T   I'd be making a bonfire out of wood, but what would I mean if I said, oh this is donkey work

p..........

Im   Miss because you have to carry it miss and you get tired miss......

boy ....and horses or donkeys....... carry things all day.......

girl..........

T   ...... so if I say that something's 'donkey work', and I might be carrying something and I might be thinking it's very...

girl hard

p   heavy

T   hard, but does it mean I've got to go and get a donkey?

pp   no...

Here is an opportunity to draw the children's attention explicitly to the figurative meaning of *donkeywork* in contrast to the meaning of *housework*. The children are led to agreement with the teacher about the meaning of each compound word without attending to the figurative behaviour of *donkey*. As well as behaving figuratively, compound words in English conceal a complex variety of implied particles: *workhouse* may be equivalent to 'a house for work'; *dinnertime* – time for dinner; *housework* may be equivalent to 'work in the house'; *bedroom* – room with bed/s. By drawing a contrast between the behaviours of these compounds and the figurative behaviour of *donkeywork*, the teacher will help to alert EAL children to their need to query meanings of compound words.

Imran shows a particularly keen interest in exploring word-meanings in this fashion. In the next extract children are invited to consult dictionaries and thesauri. Imran (Im) eagerly dives in:

T   We're looking especially for another word instead of work, not a word that goes with *hard* but another word instead of work.

[Interval]...........

Im ...found it! Miss I've found it

T   You've found it. Can you read it out to us?

Im [reads] Something that you have to do that needs a lot of energy. Reading is hard work. Two [he reads numeral].....a person's job. Has dad gone to work yet the something.....produced by work. the teacher marks our work..Four. [reads numeral]....at work, working.. a work of art..a painting. a.....[T prompts] sculpture. e. t. c. [he reads the letters].

T   etcetera

Im [reads] etcetera. Works. A factory. The moving parts of a machine.....

T   So did that tell us another word?

Im Miss there's *work* here miss

pp miss....

T   Did that tell us another word for *work*, all those words all that section. Did it tell us another word that we can use?

g   ....

T   Yes that's another sort of work isn't it. So we could work –

R   ....

I   etcetera, miss

T   Oh, listen to Raisa a minute, [Im: etcetera..] what did you find out in your thesaurus?

R   .... job

T   So another word for *work* can be a job, did it have any other suggestions?

R   a trade.......

T   a trade

R   employment

T   employment, that's good

R   business

p   hard work

pp   .... secure.........

Im   [looking in dictionary] Miss what's this word?

T   Just a minute.......listen to what Raisa's found out

R   ....

p   working.......

T   Carrying.....which one goes with...... do they all go with hard? or do some go with *hard* better than others?

Im   hard job, miss

T   a hard job, yes

J   what about a hard plumber

Im   a hard etcetera

T   You've got your plumber, haven't you, you like your plumbers

Im   miss, a hard etcetera

T   what word is it that you're trying to say?

Im   miss, e. t. c.

T   etcetera, and do you know what etcetera means? It means, and more, and some more, it's just telling us there are more examples they could think of

R   hard employment

T   hard employment

J   what's aployment [mispronounces] mean...........

p   [laughs] appointment

T   <u>employ</u>ment, well what was the word we were looking at to start with?

Im   work

T   work

J   doctor [?]

T   We've got lots of examples of jobs now, Javed, we need to think of.... we've got <u>examples</u> but we need to think of the word work

p   .... a hard exam

girl hard to make

T   ....things that are hard to make. The word I was thinking, that was in my head at the same time, was hard *labour*

pp oh yeh/labour party

T   The labour party has got something to do with it, because the Labour Party is the party for people who......

p   work

T   Yes, when the Labour party was first thought of it was made for the people who were workers and they were called labourers. And so when you talk about labour it's a party for labourers who are workers. But we can also talk about something being hard labour which means it's very very hard work.

The children's interest in the dictionaries and thesauri is clearly not matched by the skills needed to make full use of them. This teacher noted that more work was needed to help them understand the difference between the function and format of a dictionary and those of a thesaurus, and the differences between synonyms, definitions, and contextualised examples of word usage which include a range of collocative meanings. (Dictionaries vary according to their design and so do thesauri. See Chapter Five).

As the activity continues we have an example of how a 'technical' word *district* has been misinterpreted as an already familiar word *strict*. The discussion is valuable in exposing the sort of miscomprehension which children can harbour without their own or their teacher's awareness.

[Interval...]

T   So what we got out of our dictionary and our thesaurus, we got a long list of words that went with *parish*, and we got the word called *district*.

pp ....

T   *parish* meant the same as *district*

pp ....miss.... shout at people

T   *strict* means you shout at people

pp.......

boy No miss it means if you don't do your work miss they shout at you, like-

T   strict

p   when they...... get on with their work

pp when people don't work, miss and they behave... the teachers shout at them...../ they smack em boy oh strict – it means that they're really hard, bad, horrible

T   Well the whole word was district, you took a little part of it didn't you ..... *district* [p strict] district

Im oh miss di-strict, miss is that you're not, miss you don't shout at people miss di – strict

T   What an interesting idea, that's brilliant, it's not what we were thinking of. I don't think anybody else has thought of it that's really interesting – you put 'DI' at the beginning to make it the opposite

Im Yes.

Imran's analytical approach to the meaning of district, and his persistent puzzlement over *etcetera* may be contrasted with Javed's (J) earlier guesses about word meanings. The girls in this discussion are noticeably reticent in speaking out, but they also used the dictionaries with persistence and evident enjoyment. Such group-work highlights the variety of learning styles which we will want to consider in structuring 'meaning-seeking' activities.

What I believe the two transcripts above show is that EAL children are clearly eager to explore, and in considerable detail, the way words behave to convey meanings. Guided by the framework of 'lexical behaviours' the two teachers are able, each in their own style, to draw on the children's propensities to attend to meaning in a remarkably sustained and focused manner. The two transcripts represent contrasting teaching modes: one is of a small (withdrawal) group discussion and the other of a whole class expository mode. The contrast is useful in highlighting aspects of manageability of discussion and distribution of talk (consider boy/girl; teacher/pupil; focal/incidental talk; L_1/L_2 ratios). Consider the pace of interlocution, and the 'delayed comeback' of some pupils, and compare also the length of utterance of teacher and pupils. Both scenarios provide effective devices for keeping the target lexical items in focus: word-cards handled by children, photos, 3-D models etc. Both scenarios give clear indications to children that the target items 'belong' in subject domains. Both teachers make use of requests for definitions by analogy and appeal to pupils' own experience; both attend to multiple meaning and other lexical behaviours. Observe how each of the teachers welcomes or dismisses responses, uses repair and correction techniques by repeating and re-modelling the pupils' ideas. Note the humour and play on words that both teachers employ, but note also their unconscious use of the target words with other meanings!

Both teachers present themselves as model 'meaning-seekers': they provide children with evidence of their pre-lesson research, they use dictionaries and thesauri *with* the children, and crucially, they communicate their own keen sense of interest and enjoyment in word-meaning. Neither of the teachers shares the

EAL children's home languages (there are six mother-tongues represented in this class) and we need to know whether discussion in L_1 guided by a teacher who shares the language or as a peer-group activity would produce significantly different responses. In any language, the Rich Scripting framework of lexical behaviours has the potential to give meaning-seeking activities a strategic structure. The children's responses provide us with a number of indicators which can be used to advantage in planning further work, in English and, with bilingual teacher input, in L_1. I have grouped them into three sets:

consciousness of lexical behaviour

– understanding/ lack of understanding of synonymy

– understanding/ lack of understanding of the effect of collocation in word compounds [car-house, horse-work, monkey-work]

– understanding/ lack of understanding of superordination (implications for classification skills, need for graphic mapping)

– attention/ lack of attention to morphology/root meaning

– attention/ lack of attention to homophones

– attention/ lack of attention to antonyms

learning styles

– varying willingness to take risks

– chatterboxes and thinkers

– curiosity (see 'etcetera' example)

– using personal story to 'explain' words as distinct from abstract terms or generalised examples

– spontaneity/silence (note boy/girl differences)

procedural skills

– facility with dictionary/thesaurus

– alphabetical order (need for structured exercises/ visual aids)

– using code-switching to advantage

– discussion and turn-taking

The transcripts above come from a small-scale action-research project[5] which focused on the language needs of EAL children in the specific subject areas of geography and history in Year Five. The three sets of findings are generalisable in as much as they identify several criteria for observing the performance of EAL pupils of other ages and stages of English acquisition, and for examining the effectiveness of our own teaching styles. When we are brave enough to undertake the latter, the use of audio, or better still video-recordings are, as we have seen above, highly illuminating. Additional criteria are needed, however, for observing both children's learning and our own teaching, and Fitzpatrick (1996) offers practical advice:

> Videotape makes it possible to do a more detailed analysis since it is possible to replay as many times as it takes. Audio tape does not have much of the contextual information but this can be filled in for yourself if it is your own lesson or activity which is recorded. It is easier to work on transcripts of audio tape than just to listen, but making a transcript can take up a lot of time. It may be better simply to transcribe the sections which are of particular interest for you. In any event, it is often more useful to share your observations with another person. It is sometimes difficult to stand back from a situation in which we are involved and see what we take for granted from another's point of view. And it is what we take for granted which often causes problems in communication. We must remember that when teaching, we are trying to extend the pupils' learning and language skills. When assessing learning however, we must try to ensure that the language used does not prove to be a barrier which prevents the pupils from showing the extent of their learning. (Fitzpatrick, 1996)

A Rich Scripting checklist which has been used with students in initial teacher education for the primary/early years age-range follows. It is designed to prompt conscious attention to word meanings in planning, in managing and in evaluating activities/lessons in multilingual classrooms. You may wish to use it to satisfy yourself that you are making the best use of all resources to provide a 'meaning-seeking' environment in your classroom. The checklist is designed for teachers whether they use only English or more than one language. It can be used to coordinate work in team-teaching situations and across Key Stages, and it is intended to assist in planning and implementing activities and lessons (see pages 108 and 109).

Implications for curriculum planning

Time is short for EAL learners in the UK, since the national system of schooling does not allow the extra language-learning time that many children need to keep pace with their English mother-tongue peers. UK educational policy-makers would do well to heed the large number of researchers (see, for example Cummins, 1984; Collier, 1988; Thompson and Collier, 1996) who have demonstrated that many additional language learners need, in general terms, between seven and ten years to gain peer-parity in academic usage of the target language. The benefits of any extra support (Section 11 etc.) for EAL learners will continue to be ineffectually diffused for as long as their language needs are sacrificed to mechanistic requirements of curriculum 'coverage'.

Teachers who have taken this Rich Scripting approach have found that their own heightened consciousness of word-meaning not only affects their management of learning activities but that it also draws responses from children which surprise them. Indeed, the surprise of teachers is frequently reported when, for example, young children are provided with 'big' dictionaries[6], or when they are asked to concentrate for extended periods on unpicking the meaning of figurative expressions. These kinds of 'doing' have the intrinsic reward of problem-solving which yields satisfaction in the way that more mechanistic tasks do not.

We hold dear the old Chinese maxim: 'I listen and I forget, I see and I remember, I do and I understand' which has greatly influenced educational provision in the UK. Donaldson (1978), for example, builds into her theory of children's learning the strong advocacy of 'learning by doing':

> ... the paradoxical fact is that disembedded thinking, although by definition it calls for the ability to stand back from life, yields the greatest riches when it is conjoined with doing.

Jim Cummins extends Donaldson's theory of conceptualisation in first language situations by applying the idea of contextualised meaning to additional language learning, and the soundness of these two influential theories is attested in innumerable studies. 'Doing' though, is not of itself sufficient, as Vygotsky tells us. Children rely on more expert learners (usually adults) to extend their ideas about the world and develop the linguistic resources with which to encode those ideas. 'Doing' in the classroom can miss out on the expert input that is needed when tasks allow children to persist in 'doing' without understanding, for example, filling in worksheets without detecting that they have not understood the meanings of words they read and write.

Exploring word meanings in the context of curriculum topics calls for a co-ordinated school approach. Not detecting their lack of understanding of words, or not rising to the *need* to understand words, are two root causes of under-achievement for many EAL children. Unless the culture of classrooms consistently addresses the business of word meaning this underachievement will persist.

Notes and References

1   Maggie Power's observation

2   Thankyou, Mark Stampley and children of Class 5H for this activity and the following transcript

3   Taken by a student-teacher, as it happened

4   Thankyou to Geraldine Cooper for this transcript

5   Thanks to Christine Crowther and the support of GEST II funding

6   More about dictionaries in Chapter Five.

PLANNING

In my activity/lesson planning have I

- identified English target lexical items (words and phrases) demanded by the learning focus
- identified lexical items in languages other than English
- used other sources (in English and other languages) to explore word meanings (e.g. family members, friends, colleagues)
- used an English dictionary to develop my own knowledge
- used a bilingual dictionary
- used an English thesaurus
- used a thesaurus for a language other than English?

In my activity/lesson planning have I built in opportunities to develop children's attention to word-meanings by asking for/drawing attention in appropriate ways to:

- definitions of words/phrases e.g. 'What does x mean?'
- synonyms of words/phrases e.g. 'Who can think of another word that means the same as x ?'
- cultural experience/analogies 'Imagine what it's like when you........'
- multiple meanings of words/phrases
- homophones (and near homophones, e.g. fax/facts)
- figurative expressions
- similes (e.g. as hard as nails; as clean as a whistle)
- words with different grammatical functions e.g. nouns and verbs
- words which often collocate (occur together)
- co-ordinates (... and ... e.g. to and fro; tattered and torn)
- the root/affixes of words
- word compounds
- idiomatic/clichéd phrases ('chunks' e.g. it's a small world; mind how you go)
- proverbs (many hands make light work; too many cooks spoil the broth)
- translations and L_1/English equivalents
- the derivation/origin of words/phrases?

Thinking about children's active curiosity about word-meanings, have I planned ways for children to operate in L_1 and in English:

- to ask me about words/phrases
- to ask each other about words/phrases
- to ask their families about words/phrases
- to use dictionaries to explore word-meanings (not just check spellings)
- to use thesauri to explore word-meanings
- to learn and use alphabetical order
- to express their own cultural associations/analogies
- to distinguish literal and figurative meanings of words/phrases?

Have I planned to use English or other languages in:

- phonological awareness activities (alliteration and assonance, rhyme, onset and rime)
- jokes involving play on words (e.g. making joke books)

- brainstorming word-meanings for poetry
- graphic (i.e. word-shape) poetry on paper/on computer
- teacher (me) using a dictionary or thesaurus in the classroom
- imaging (e.g. 'tell me what you see in your head/tell me how you feel when you think of x')
- classroom displays/mobiles of words/phrases
- using glossaries for topic work
- cloze procedure activities – in pairs and small groups/on computer
- using newspapers for word-meaning activities
- using environmental print (e.g. street signs, adverts)
- bringing words from home
- classifying superordinates and hyponyms (e.g. furniture [superordinate]: table, chair, cupboard etc [hyponyms])
- quizzes about word meanings (*not* word-searches!)?

How will I, the teacher, as model meaning-seeker:

- develop my own consciousness of word-meanings
- extend my range of vocabulary in English
- extend my range of vocabulary in languages other than English
- develop my classroom as a word-rich environment that stimulates inquiry into word-meanings
- present myself to children as a model meaning-seeker
- present myself as someone who enjoys words because they are funny and intriguing and powerful and...?

IMPLEMENTATION

The attention of EAL learners to lexical meaning in curriculum topics depends firstly on teacher consciousness of lexical behaviours, and secondly on teacher management of children's attention to those behaviours. Some strategies are particularly effective:

- regular use of devices for keeping the target words/phrases in focus
- giving clear indications to children that the target items 'belong' in subject domains
- frequent requests for definitions, analogies, multiple meaning (including figurative), appeal to pupils' own experience and home languages, synonyms
- welcoming responses, with repair and correct modelling
- allowing for 'delayed comeback' of more reticent pupils
- humour and play on words
- non-verbal strategies, including mime
- shared 'imaging' in checking on common construction of meanings
- presenting self as model 'meaning-seeker', by using dictionaries in classroom *with* the children, by providing children with evidence of pre-lesson research (including rich scripting), by communicating own enthusiasm for words.

- adopting a style of questioning and response which encourages risk-taking
- orchestrating frequent repetition, but not assuming that the teacher's own repetition of the target lexemes 'does the job'.

Chapter Four

Cultural belonging

A colleague relates how excited a group of children were when their tadpoles changed into frogs and how they took one small green creature to show their Headteacher. They watched as she lifted it up, stroked it and then kissed it. There was a moment of awe-struck silence – and then one child whispered:

'Try it again miss, it doesn't always work first time'[1].

Teachers of EAL pupils know that the 'entitlements' of the National Curriculum present particular challenges. EAL pupils are not only developing conceptually, they are also acquiring cultural knowledge which in many ways differs from the cultural ideas attached to their mother-tongue – the language of their family and immediate community. Their academic achievement depends not only on their communicative competence in English but also on their willingness to engage with cultural dimensions of the language through which the school curriculum is imparted. Cultural engagement is one of the determining factors in successful language learning, and when EAL learners engage with the cultural aspects of lexical meaning, they are better equipped to progress through the curriculum successfully. Young EAL learners need to know how words relate to knowledge about their world and need to negotiate new meanings by making connections with their stored world knowledge, some of which will be drawn from cultural and linguistic schemas that teachers do not share. If meaning-negotiation processes are to be effective, the learning milieu must be culturally inclusive: learners must feel that they belong in the classroom so they must have a share in the control of meaning-seeking. All teachers, and particularly those who do not share EAL pupils' home repertoire, need to develop their own consciousness of the ways in which language affects cultural belonging.

Where meanings are drawn from a closely shared cultural or experiential repertoire, it might be expected that a high degree of rapport exists in the mental imaging of both parties, though we may never know how to prove this. To some extent we are able to, and in everyday life frequently do check our assumptions of this rapport by various means of negotiation. Communication involves many lexical items (words and phrases) which depend for their meaning on cultural referencing. When cultural experiences are closely allied to a different language, it makes sense to use that language to explore the references. Use of L_1 by children, and by teachers who share their repertoire, will enhance the collective referencing. Many English lexical items – polysemes, figurative expressions and the like – provide a choice of possible and/or probable meanings. Reference to L_1 equivalents will not only help to clarify the intended meaning needed for learning the curriculum but, crucially, they will affirm the role of home and community culture in the learning process.

When making links between language and culture we teachers may forget to ask ourselves: What is culture? No neatly definitive answer exists; many of the mistakes of 'multicultural education' are due to over-simplistic interpretations of cultural differences. The question is one which needs to be addressed in inclusive and challenging ways, so that the multilingual classroom is seen as a collection of cultural differences continually evolving and interacting with each other, rather than as a set of cultural divisions set to oppose each other.

Cultural belonging is not a romantic, cosy notion – a means of making children feel 'happy' in school while ignoring the wider context of social inequalities. On the contrary, we must be alert to the role of language in what Cummins (1996) calls the '*coercive* power relations' of our social systems and which he contrasts with pupils' sense of cultural and linguistic identity arising from a school ethos of '*collaborative* power':

> Power is created *with* others rather than being imposed on or exercised over others... students whose schooling experiences reflect collaborative relations of power develop the ability, confidence and motivation to succeed academically... They feel a sense of ownership for the learning that goes on in the classroom and a sense that they belong in the classroom learning community. (Cummins, 1996)

Cultural and academic empowerment is underpinned by a school ethos which uses language and languages as a means of strengthening children's identities. Word-meaning exploration which crosses language boundaries is part of each learner's negotiation of identity.

Haastrup (1991) reports on processes of 'negotiating meaning' in which older EFL learners are led to infer the meanings of English lexical units not in syntactic relations but by reference to L_1-related cultural knowledge. These 'lexical inferencing procedures' are seen by Haastrup as a source of theoretical understanding of learner strategies and also as an element of L_2 teaching methodology, and she recognises the advantages for both teacher and learner to engage with word meaning:

> ... meaning does not lie exclusively in the code as meaning potential, but is developed in interaction with the users of that code. (Haastrup,1991)

The implications here, says Haastrup are for world knowledge 'in the form of schematic or conceptual knowledge' to feature prominently in accessing the target language and for linguistic competence to take account of cultural competence in both L_1 and L_2.

Foreign language teaching in the UK shows similar neglect of lexical meaning in relation to culture. Byram (1992) expresses anxiety about the way languages are taught in the UK as though pupils would use them merely as tourists:

> This has no effect on their view of their own identity and that of others; they are implicitly invited to remain firmly anchored in their own values and culture (Byram, 1992).

In much the same way, but with different consequences, I fear that many EAL pupils are excluded from the connotative dimensions of linguistic meaning. If teachers do not involve EAL pupils in constructing word-meanings that relate to cross-cultural experiences, their 'belonging' to English will be severely limited.

Just as linguistic knowledge is both a goal and a barrier, so is cultural knowledge, but it is often not recognised as either.[2]

– A history teacher points to a picture of a well saying, 'That's like the wells in Pakistan.'

'No it's not, miss. There aren't any.'

– A geography teacher displays a picture of the Himalayan foothills: 'Have you ever seen snow like this in your country?'

'No, 'cos it's all mucky here.'

How do we enter into cultural enquiry *with* children in ways which 'affirm their developing sense of self' (Cummins, 1996), and which avoid impositions of stereotyped and static cultural images while at the same time furthering their knowledge of the world?

For the teacher, the key question about words used with children in the multilingual classroom is: what range of images may we share with each other? **Shared imaging** is a way of talking about what connotations words trigger for each of us. It is a process which involves all parties in reconstruction – the speaker reconstructing a set of mental images as a verbal text and the audience reconstructing a mental/sensory set from the words they hear. As teachers, we need to inquire how words affect the imaging of learners and maintain awareness that common usage of words can mask differences in the meanings which learners construct. This cultural meaning-seeking persists into advanced stages of additional language acquisition. A visitor from the former communist state of Bulgaria, highly fluent in English, was baffled by the free movement of sheep on the Yorkshire fells even after it was explained to him how farmers leave their flocks to mingle on the hills and cooperate each spring in bringing them down and sorting them according to their ear-tags he remained puzzled. Talking earlier with English colleagues, his stereotyped ideas about private profiteering and competitive industry in Western Europe had been very evident, so his hosts attributed his continued puzzlement to his inability to imagine that the farmers might cooperate. Some time elapsed before the visitor tried again: 'And do the shepherds have to go out and find their own sheep each day for milking?'

Here is an assertive and effective adult language-learner who is not afraid to pursue his non-comprehension, in spite of the gap in cultural knowledge which prevented his native English-speaking 'teacher' from understanding his non-understanding. The cultural gap occurred because the English teacher did not know about the Bulgarian tradition of rearing sheep for their milk, and the non-comprehension was only resolved because the learner was eager and comfortable enough to persist in satisfying his cultural curiosity. It is unfortunately far more common for younger EAL learners in school either not to see the need to acquire the cultural meanings upon which many curriculum topics are based, or to settle for a low grade of understanding without drawing attention to it.

> One word or phrase can hold the key to meaning of a whole piece of discourse. A colleague relates how an American lecturer at a conference in Poland was describing the need for a 'crap-detector' in curriculum policy-making. The word sent fluent translators into a flurry of discussion and uncertainty as they settled unhappily for the Polish equivalent of *crab*...[3]

Acculturalisation

Early acculturalisation sets the scene for our meaning-seeking. In infancy everything that we see, hear, touch, taste, smell, can be explored, and not only with our eyes, our ears, our skin, our tongues and our noses – we find that there is another means of making sense of the world. There is language. Those around us, our 'significant others' have the power too. They can ask us questions. They make us answer, they make us think. We think to each other as we talk to each other. And together we organise our seeing, our hearing, our touching, our tasting and our smelling. We organise our perceptions, our questions and our answers. If as small children we are encouraged by the responses that we get, we ask and keep on asking, and patterns begin to emerge. We learn most readily about that which we perceive as significant. The heuristics of language use is culturally filtered.

By degrees, our understandings and experiences are encoded. In very large measure we agree to use the same coding system of denotation, of reference and explanation that our 'significant others' use. We agree about words, about intonation, grammar, discourse structure. We develop sensitivity to register appropriate to different semantic fields. If we are bilingual or bidialectal we learn to code-switch according to our audience and the context and purpose of the discourse.

The pattern may be particularly rich. We may turn to a parent and exchange in a code called Panjabi, to an auntie using a code called Urdu, to a friend and it's Mirpuri, to a book and find English, to television and meet Australian or American English. And as meanings are exchanged, explored, agreed and stored, each code acquires substance, shape, texture and temperature, tone, colour and scent. Our linguistic repertoire flourishes. As it grows so too does our mental imagery – sounds, scents, pictures, feelings – collected 'items', as Stevick (1986) calls them, from the thousand-and-one encounters of everyday life – trivial and routine, noteworthy and uncommon, stored and referenced.

Our understanding becomes a process of matching words with the imaging that informs our thinking. We must alter or add to our stored images many times before we confidently grasp ideas which invite our attention but demand that we risk discomforting our prior labels and classifications. Binary opposites must give way to ranking and relativism, to juxtaposition and paradox; categories must be re-negotiated and compromised; cause and effect is over-ruled. We talk. We talk to find meanings in the world, to add meanings to the world.

Imaging, which encompasses reference to all our perceptions, furnishes our meaning-seeking. As we learn new language we must fit it into schemata of multi-sensory experience. We must make links between our personae, our lives and the language we encounter by weaving the words and phrases into a nexus of connotation which ranges from the deeply private to that shared by family, community and other more public groups, some of which invite and support our right of participation, some of which are hostile to us. To belong culturally we must claim shares of ownership in the connotative discourse which surrounds us, and if we do not participate with sufficient commitment to its dynamics, we are excluded.

Our dependence on emotional, physical, social, economic, intellectual, aesthetic, moral 'others' can significantly shape our metalinguistic awareness before schooling even begins to play its part. By the time we begin school we have propensities of perception and interpretation closely linked to our linguistic and cultural experience. As we allow the complexities of life to filter through to our consciousness, each of us unique in our pattern of experiences and relationships, we are drawn into a dazzling world of discourse. Words we have come to use confidently to label, become opaque or tinged with 'otherness', or startle us with new significance in new contexts. We must repeatedly re-negotiate their meanings as we meet them in conversations with our elders, pick them out of the flow of TV talk or from adults talking to each other, and drink them greedily in from stories told and read to us. Our cultural grounding, always in some measure unique, is weighted by the company we keep.

Meaning-making continues through childhood into adulthood. I have happily used the word *colorado* in Spanish in a domestic domain for years to talk about matching socks, about sunsets and the like, or maybe to note somebody's embarrassment or exertion, and the word for me belongs in such scenarios. In a quite separate domain, the word *Colorado* has been a label (note the use of capital C) I have used for a river marked on the map of America, studied long ago in an English medium classroom.. As with countless other words, multiple meanings accrue from multiple contexts. My two domains of *colorado* have held apart my privately stored meanings for the word. It is useful to draw attention to the fact that I had absolutely no problem with the two separated ways of manipulating the word.

Then recently I took a walk far enough into the depths of the Grand Canyon to catch a glimpse of this river whose label I had so often used. The sight was momentarily disconcerting: I realised that my imaging of the river had all these years been at odds with how it was perceived by other people who also use the label *Colorado*. Instead of bright, sparkling water reflecting the sun and adding light to the reddish-brown rocks, I saw a reddish-brown flow, so dark that it appeared to be a part of the rocks, resembling no other river I have ever seen. The meaning of *Colorado* immediately acquired a force of congruence with my *colorado*, and my membership of that cultural/linguistic group which can manipulate *colorado* was dramatically and memorably affected. The noun-label *colorado*, hitherto of purely denotative force, now has for me a semantic weighting of which I was unaware, about which I had never felt the need to negotiate nor been invited to do so.

I had *never felt the need to negotiate, nor been invited to do so...* and long into adulthood my usage of *colorado* has been restricted. Asking children in multilingual classrooms to 'image' is asking them to attend consciously to their cultural experience and perceptions. Asking them to share their images is asking them to contribute to the construction of a shared cultural framework which promotes collaborative meaning-seeking.

Michael Halliday (1978) invokes Mary Douglas (1971) in locating the relationship between language and culture:

> If we ask of any form of communication the simple question 'what is being communicated?' the answer is: information from the social system. The exchanges which are being communicated constitute the social system. (Halliday, 1978)

How do we 'share' our streets, for example? Who belongs, in the meanings of *Mecca* and *profit/prophet*?

With any group of children a teacher needs to make judgements about prior linguistic and cultural knowledge which may be assumed and built upon, but where the linguistic repertoire of teacher and children is not highly concurrent attention to cultural content in word meaning needs to be proportionally greater. In multilingual classrooms we will meet pupils whose linguistic repertoire is different from our own, and even if we share some of our pupils' home languages we are aware that the age-gap contributes to differences in cultural perception and interpretation.

For some children living in close-knit communities, schooling may be the main context for direct contact with English-speaking adults. As children expand their vocabulary they use words with increasingly complex intentionality. What becomes important is not only adding more and more words but also re-working the meanings of known words which behave polysemously and operating them in a variety of contexts. Young EAL learners have plenty of practice in doing this in L_1 where their interaction with adults provides support and extension of meanings, but it is very much harder to work all this out in English when contact with adult models is limited.

Viv Edwards (1986) examines the relationship between social interaction and linguistic repertoire in a black Birmingham community. She observes friendship patterns among black patois speakers and their relevance to the choices young bilinguals make about which language they use with whom:

> Life chances open to young black people predispose them to spending more of their time in the company of other black people than in the company of whites. Patterns of settlement imposed on the availability of work and the level of income mean that most black people live in areas where there is a high ethnic minority population. Friendships based on a given locality are necessarily strengthened when schools are organized on a neighbourhood basis... It is largely academic to speculate on the degree to which such friendships are based on choice or result from structural factors... (Edwards 1986)

However well disposed a teacher is towards multilingualism, EAL children know that power resides out there with groups different from themselves and their families. So talk about it! To ignore racism is to collude with it. School is not a haven from life, it is part of life and of societal power structures that children must cope with.

Fitzpatrick (1987) reports how keen parents are for their children to learn and maintain their mother-tongue while wanting also them to acquire full command of English. Many parents will resist the erosion of cultural values they hold dear and so restrict those aspects of their children's social interaction they see as potentially damaging to the cohesion of traditional family and community values. Racism may inhibit patterns of interaction between EAL learners and English mother-tongue peer groups, and ethnic minority perception of 'English' culture be shaped more by the mass media than by sustained human relationships. Inevitably, many of our young bilinguals are growing up with a facility of English which lacks deep-rooted affiliation. Patterns of linguistic repertoire change rapidly, though, in successive generations, as inter-cultural contact presents children with options and dilemmas their parents have not themselves experienced.

Children respond to role models with whom they identify, and it is natural for children to wish to see themselves reflected in their teachers. Student-teachers of South-Asian origin, for example, whose physical appearance is akin to that of their pupils and their pupils' families, have reported with evident pride about the rapport they are able to establish in multilingual classrooms. Even very young children 'know' that physical characteristics may entail other cultural characteristics and there is a particular delight in seeing young ethnic minority children respond to a teacher whom they recognise as 'like themselves'. But it is not automatically the case that similarity of physical appearance concurs with the important cultural detail of children's lives, nor is it at all the case that distinct physical appearance determines 'otherness'. Children's responses to their teachers are as complex as any human relationships and the picture is certainly not black and white!

Crossing linguistic boundaries

One student-teacher of Gujerati heritage was perplexed by a young Muslim child's enthusiastic assumption that she could read Urdu, and did not know how to respond to his emergent writing in the Perso-Arabic script without disappointing him; students whose use of spoken Panjabi is fluent in domestic and social contexts are anxious about gaps in their vocabulary when they apply their home language to academic subjects; white English mother-tongue students feel rebuffed when their first attempts at using children's home languages are met with giggles.

When we teach children whose languages we don't know, or don't know as well as we might wish, all of us are personally and professionally challenged. I believe it is vital to respond with:
  – respect
  – warmth
  – curiosity
  – good humour
  – commitment to learn.

Our knowledge about lexical behaviours provides a framework for asking questions about languages we don't know and making connections between curriculum discourse and children's lives. The word *background* is inappropriate. Only if we take the teacher or the curriculum as the focal concern of education can a child's life be considered as 'background'. In effect, when we bring home languages into the learning process we *foreground* children's identities. This crucial point is made by Cummins (1996):

> When students' developing sense of self is affirmed and extended through their interactions with teachers, they are more likely to apply themselves to academic effort. The more we learn, the more we want to learn, and the more effort we are prepared to put into that learning.

> By contrast, when students' language, culture and experience are ignored or excluded in classroom interactions, students are immediately starting from a disadvantage. Everything they have learned about life and the world up to this point is being dismissed as irrelevant to school learning; there are few points of connection to curriculum materials or instruction and so students are expected to learn in an experiential vacuum. Students' silence and non-participation under these conditions have frequently been interpreted as lack of academic ability or effort, and teachers' interactions with students have reflected a pattern of low expectations which have become self-fulfilling (Cummins, 1996).

Effective participation in shared meaning-making indicates *belonging* to the linguistic/cultural group which creates and controls the patterns and purposes of the discourse. Individuals can gauge their access to group discourse – ranging from exclusion, through degrees of restricted participation, to degrees of active contribution. The stronger their status of belonging, the more they are able to represent their experience of belonging to the group by employing a shared lexicon.

The degree of congruence between an individual's control of lexical items and their set of perceptions about the world, in whatever sphere of culture (religion, sport, plumbing, knock-knock jokes...), provides an indication of their 'belonging status' in that group. So, 'experts' are acknowledged, par excellence, according to their ability and *willingness* to contribute and communicate in the group. Whether or not they are always the best qualified people to do so is not the question: what matters is that their interpretations of the topic have the potential to affect the reality of the topic. Outsiders, or fringe members of the group, on the other hand, will typically display limitations in their manipulation of the 'in' language of the topic and/or lack of influence in defining it. A 'culture' (or sub-culture) then, relies on a repertoire of representation for its survival and cohesion, and prime among these is the linguistic substantiation of its ideas. The discourse of classrooms does more than *represent* the knowledge and skills of the topic in hand. It defines the *belonging* of the knowledge and skills.

Topics and activities which put 'subject' knowledge into a framework of negotiation provide some of the best contexts for language learning, and the benefits of attention to word meaning are cumulative when teachers and children share in processes of imaging. Learners who contribute to collective imaging of word-meanings by drawing on their L_1 related connotations are better able to construct their individual semantic maps and negotiate appropriate matches for their personal word meanings with those of the teacher and other people.

When looking for **synonyms** (or near synonyms), EAL learners should always be encouraged to refer to L_1, not settle for bland, over-used equivalents but search for evocative, expressive forms: e.g. equivalents of *hue* rather than *colour*; equivalents of *like a bat out of hell* instead of *very fast*; equivalents of *vast, colossal* instead of *very big*.

> Names are imbued with cultural significance. Studying the meanings of names and naming conventions across different languages gives pupils opportunities to re-assert their own name-form and their knowledge of their country of family heritage (and very often to point out mispronunciation or other errors).
>
> - names of people and forms of address
>
> - male /female markers (and indication of marital status)
>
> a   diminutives
>
> - place names (also streets, houses)
>   history (Beckfoot, Shuttleworth Street)
>   connotations (Wuthering Heights)
>
> - brand names
>   connotations
>   acronyms

Children's ability to make rich and astute associations of words, images and experience depends on a wide range of vocabulary in English and in L_1. So the target lexical items we include in our lesson/activity planning will include the nouns, adjectives, verbs and adverbs which most effectively evoke multi-sensory cultural associations. Some words can seem to be closely related in meaning but have important differences in connotation.

smile.. smirk.. grin ...
look.. glance ...
walk.. stroll ...
run.. hurtle ...

Some words appear 'neutral'; others are 'marked'

- He *went* off/gallivanted off

- She *sat* in the chair/slumped in the chair

- He *told* her he that would come/promised her that he would come

Some words seem to belong to **scales** of meaning, e.g. *tasty*

boring..ok..nice..tasty..delicious..exquisite..

try building a scale around these:

...awful...
...enormous...
...warm...
...fascinating...

Some words/phrases **imply** meanings which they do not actually state. For example:

*He **accused** me...* implies that something undesirable has occurred.
*We **repaired** the car...* implies that the car was damaged.

Look at the implication in

- *respond*
- *release*
- *manage*

We use numerous expressions without noticing that they are culturally acquired. Many of these use the **simile** forms *as...as...* or *like*:

as easy as pie   *like a bat out of hell*
as old as the hills   *like peas in a pod*

All languages have words for sets, which are culturally derived. In English some of them are used to indicate a number of animals, but they can also be used for effect, for example:

- a *herd* of football fans
- a *gaggle* of schoolkids.

Our awareness of the cultural loading of English lexical items prompts us to draw children's attention to them while we are teaching, so that they develop an atunement to both the heritage and to the currency of such expressions. Researching equivalents in L_1 will alert children to semantic subtleties which they otherwise miss. **Archaisms** abound in English, many of them traceable to biblical origins, Shakespeare or other literary influences:

writ large
blot your copybook
and ne'er the twain shall meet
let bygones be bygones
seen the light
sword of Damocles
Achilles' heel
woe betide...

Homilies will be found to have their equivalents in other languages:

prevention is better than cure
do as you would be done by
honesty is the best policy
I beg your pardon
where there's a will there's a way.

Children's encounters with idiomatic lexical units (proverbs, homilies, figurative expressions) acculturalise them in ways which strengthen their identity. Lack of facility in English idiom will prevent them from participating and contributing to whole areas of discourse. In L_1 idiom becomes a source of power when it is transferred from domestic usage to academic learning. A classroom climate which promotes the negotiation of word meanings will benefit young EAL learners who are continually faced with 'texts' composed of denotative and figurative lexical items, weighted by a cultural framework they have not inherited directly through family ... but to which they belong by their rights in a social system. Teachers who don't share their children's home language need to attend to their own knowledge, skills, attitudes (affective, cultural, political etc.) about language and learning, bilingual development, self-concept and culture. Teachers who do, in whatever measure, share that home language need to do the same, but from different vantage points. The fact that a teacher's linguistic repertoire matches that of the child is not of itself enough. Each teacher needs to balance their own cultural heritage with a cultural currency that children may identify with.

A teacher explained her preferred image of *pushing up the daisies* as Jesus *brushing* up the daisies. Other expressions in the same vein need some explaining too!

fall off your perch	pass away
snuff it	give up the ghost
pop off	kick the bucket
pop your clogs	pass on /away

Currency of lexical units is one measure of history. When we watch old TV broadcasts we are struck not only by the accents but also by the old-fashioned 'turn of phrase' of speakers in newscasts, films, interviews. You can almost 'translate' some of the utterances into present day equivalents but other expressions remain robust in contemporary discourse. TV and radio recordings provide excellent resources for developing pupils' consciousness of idiom and metaphor. If we heighten their consciousness they will be able to find many more instances during their own viewing of TV, including films in home language.

Idiomatic phrases of a speech community are used long beyond their epoch of cultural 'truth'. Many expressions have 'literal' meanings that are opaque, especially to children and adult EAL learners. This is true for all languages, each of which has its own innumerable idiomatic and formulaic expressions. The archaism of some expressions may if anything increase their communicative effect, and using them is a marker of a speaker's cultural affinity. This is apparent when comparing the discourse of native speakers with that of fluent adult speakers in, for example, multinational contexts where 'international English' is the *lingua franca*. Metaphors, in any language, are culturally acquired. In a rapidly changing technological society new metaphors are coined and others become rapidly archaic or opaque, particularly to children:

> like peas in a pod
> like taking coals to Newcastle
> like looking for a needle in a haystack

With other kinds of cultural change – ecological, political, medical, sporting etc. – other expressions may, in time, serve as glimpses of a cultural heritage rather than having present-day currency:

> there are plenty more fish in the sea
> you can't see the wood for the trees
> it never rains but it pours
> I can feel it in my bones
> I smell a rat
> the pecking order
> back to square one

How about researching the stories in these phrases ...

- dog in a manger
- ugly duckling
- tablets of stone
- pound of flesh

The **derivation** of words may be part of dictionary exploration and part of attending to spelling. Many words in English owe their apparently irregular spelling to their historical connection with other languages:

debt

doubt

reign

rough

All the teaching ideas in this book directed at EAL learners are, I show throughout, equally valid for English mother-tongue pupils. All children should understand that languages borrow from each other and that words we take for granted as 'English' reflect a history of contact with speakers of other languages over the centuries, for instance:

words from Greek:
crisis museum telephone orchestra cycle chorus acrobat alphabet

words from Latin:
recipe circus school January street giant fungus album exit

words from Hindi:
chutney bangle dungarees pyjamas shampoo yoga bungalow catamaran

Words from Norwegian and Danish:
take hit sister husband fellow outlaw saga skill root wing wrong

Words from Celtic languages:
shamrock macintosh whisky jockey loch down galore

Words from French:
artist ballet procession restaurant bureau garage avalanche balloon

Words from Dutch:
deck scone waggon landscape luck boss hope skipper

(*Source*: 'Our Word House Game' in Fisher and Hicks, 1985)

So what is the English word for *pizza*?

Salience

Despite teachers' intentions, children acquire and communicate meanings vicariously, idiosyncratically, and erroneously. Culture as a societal pheno-menon is always made more complex by the individual's experiences. Although they are influenced by patterns of transmitted culture, children will also show individual responses to the linguistic demands made on them according to the **salience** words and ideas have for them. A ten-year-old appears not to know the meaning of *transform,* yet has a collection of Transformer toys that turn from cars into robots[4]. We may use lexical chunks without recognising their cultural oddities. A teacher found that (English mother-tongue) children in her year five class understood *white as a sheet* as 'white as a **sheep**'. But then children's sheets are not often white these days!

A collection of children's writing about Christmas reveals the wide range of interpretations children can put on stories. These sentences are from the work of children at a Wakefield primary school:

- a long time ago Mary and Joseph off to bethlehem to lay a baby (6 yrs)

- Joseph said to Mary who you have got a big tummy I think you are going to have a baby. I think I am said Mary and then she hatched it. (8 yrs)

- the shepherds crept up to the stabul and peed round the door Oh said Mary do come in. (8 yrs)

- Herod sent out some men. He sed if you see eney americans on camels bring them to me, but they came back and sed there are no americans in camels. (8 yrs)

- During the night a baby was born. Mary and Joseph found out it was their baby so they called him Jesus and Jesus grew up to be a healthy young man but unfortunately he was put on a cross. A really big cross. (8 yrs)

- Joseph. 'come on Mary lets set of for Bethleyheym'
  Mary 'I can't be going to Bethleyheym I'm pregnant' (8 yrs)

- They followed a star until they came to a stable and crowded round jesus and sang hymns for a bit. (8 yrs)

- Jesus was born in Bethlehem. His father was could Joseph he was a caterpillar (8 yrs)

- In the night Jesus was born. Mary woke up and towld Joseph. he woke up and said oh luck its a boy (8 yrs).

'Alive and Kicking' Saturday TV show
Meena, age 9, is a contestant in a quiz.
The question is:
    Is Beethoven
    a) a dog
    b) deaf
    c) a composer?

Meena answers a) and is clearly confused when the compère tells her she is wrong. A film by the title of 'Beethoven' about a big sloppy dog of the same name has only recently been shown on TV.

Literacy in L_1

Literacy is the bedrock of EAL children's bilingualism, extending their linguistic competence beyond transactional, domestic domains to the realms of academic and cognitively demanding usage. Heritage languages will lack strength for future cultural transmission if literacy skills are neglected. Consequently any serious support for multilingualism needs to include support for children's reading and writing in L_1. It seems to me unnecessary to rehearse the cognitive and cultural benefits of literacy – we would not be in teaching if we did not believe in them. But it is surprising that many teachers 'block' their professional understanding of the importance of literacy when they consider it in relation to languages other than English. Everything that Cummins (1984 and subsequently) has to say about the 'common underlying proficiency' of bilingualism applies to literacy skills as much as, indeed more than, oracy skills. Reading and writing demand a far greater lexical repertoire than our common patterns of spoken discourse, and many of the cognitive benefits of literacy events transfer between L_1 and L_2 and vice versa. In practice, a little knowledge of the written form of our pupils' languages can do much to support their L_1 literacy, although full command can do much more. What I want to stress is that we need not be afraid of languages we don't know – we can learn as much as we want to of any language, and the more pupils see us working at it, the more we confirm our commitment to their cultural identity. By learning a little about how home languages are written we make an all-important statement to our pupils: I want to know you.

Just as we use a framework of lexical behaviours in English to inquire into languages we don't know, so we can find out about how words are written down (orthography) in those languages by revisiting the basis of English orthography. We may be particularly daunted by unfamiliar scripts such as Arabic, Devanagri, Cyrillic or Hebrew, or, baffled by the many different conventions used in Roman script that English employs in such diverse languages as Turkish, Swedish, Portuguese. As literate adults we already have the tools of inquiry, but we may need to re-activate our consciousness of them. Here, colleagues who have learned to read and write in a language that has a different orthography have an advantage over those whose literacy is confined to English. Teachers of young children, however, are well placed to apply their knowledge of phoneme-grapheme correspondence in English to languages they don't know. Under-standing that squiggles on paper represent sounds that come out of our mouths is a massive conceptual discovery that we all made many years ago. We don't need to relearn this concept when we tackle unfamiliar orthographies, but it helps to take a fresh look at the job these squiggles do.

The orthographies of languages we are likely to encounter in UK classrooms fall basically into three types – alphabetic, syllabic and logographic.[5] All use marks on paper to represent sounds (although logographic languages such as Chinese languages also use characters to represent ideas and therefore serve multiple phoneme-grapheme correspondence). All are systematic and learnable (small children all over the world manage them!). As with the English examples I have used to illustrate lexical behaviours, I will limit illustration of graphophonic behaviour to a collection of features that English displays. Readers and writers of other languages will be able to apply the same principles to explore how other writing systems represent the spoken words. I recommend that you start by using 'simple' lexical units – words for objects, say, rather than sentence units – so that you concentrate on the correspondence of spoken and written forms and not the grammar.

Learn from children and parents how to write their names. Use roman-letter transliteration to help you to match sounds and symbols.

Phonemes and graphemes

When we speak words, we use sounds which we call phonemes. Phonemes are the smallest units of sound that contribute to the meaning of a word, such that the meaning of the word is affected if we change one or more of them by substitution, addition or omission. It is hard to represent this idea on paper because the spellings of words interfere with our attention to their sound when spoken. Try to ignore the spellings of these examples and speak them out loud to pick out the change of phoneme in each pair:

1. *cat* – 3 phonemes. Change the first phoneme to make – bat

2. *bat* – 3 phonemes. Change the second phoneme to make – bait

3. *bait* – 3 phonemes. Change the third phoneme to make – bale

4. *bale* – 3 phonemes. Add a phoneme in second position to make – Braille

5. *Braille* – 4 phonemes. Change the fourth phoneme to make – brate

6. *brate* – 4 phonemes. Omit the first phoneme to make – rate

7. *rate* – 3 phonemes. Change the third phoneme to make – reign

8. *reign* – 3 phonemes. Change the second phoneme to make – rin.

Remember, it is the change of sound which causes the change in the meaning of each word when spoken. Only one phoneme has been changed in each pair. You will have noticed in 5. and 8. that the change in phoneme results in words that you don't recognise (when you hear them) as meaningful in English – you, of course, being a fluent adult user of English, whether or not as your first language. Examples 5 and 8 sound like English words, but you can't attach a meaning to them. The difference of just one phoneme results in these 'meaningless' words.

Some of the spellings I have chosen to represent these words on the page influence the meanings you attach to them as you read them, for example in *reign*. I could have written *rain* or *rein* or, for that matter, *rane* or *wrain*. But we're not considering spelling yet because phonemes are units of sound which contribute to the meaning of words when they are spoken, so don't be led to a meaning by the way I have written the words. The sounds we use when saying *bat* or *reign*, for example, can already convey more than one meaning in English as well as different meanings in other languages, before we spell them differently for different meanings. Say the following words out loud and see how this works for you:

pownd   *kee*   *wryte*   *phaire*   *greighter*

How we represent the sounds of words on paper depends on which orthographic system we choose to use, and I have chosen to use letters of the roman alphabet in ways that you will recognise as 'English' spelling patterns. But note that the number of phonemes in a word does not have to correspond with the number of letters, nor with the number of syllables. To write the words down I had to use a grapheme for each phoneme. Some are formed with one letter of the roman alphabet, as in *cat* and *bat*, i.e. three graphemes each; others with two or more letters of the roman alphabet, like the *ai* in *bait*, and the *ll* in *Braille*. It is easy to recognise how a two-letter grapheme formed with letters that sit next to each other matches up with the phoneme it represents. It is not quite so easy to see the phoneme-grapheme correspondence where a two-letter grapheme is split so that, for example, the a and e form one sound: *bale, brate, rate* and *arrane*.

The way we pronounce words affects the meanings they convey and/or the meanings taken by listeners. Accents cause the sound of words to vary without intending a change of meaning, but this can affect the hearer's understanding if they are not familiar with the characteristic sounds of the accent. Try the following words, first in a Cockney accent and then a Yorkshire accent:

glass
Grant (of *East Enders'* fame)
know
butter
fine

If you are familiar with both of these English accents, you won't have a problem understanding that the word-meanings stay the same even though the pronunciation varies. You know that change of accent is different from change of phoneme. But this is not nearly so obvious if you are listening to an unfamiliar accent, even in your first language. And it is more likely to strain your understanding if you are listening to an unfamiliar accent in an additional language.

When we write words in English, the graphemes used to represent the sounds of the spoken words are standardised as spellings and so do not represent variety of spoken accent. Nor do they represent intonation or stress. Teachers of young children who are at the stage of 'semi-phonetic' spelling will often see children trying to match letter sounds or letter names to their own individual way of pronouncing a word. The child has to realise that this doesn't work, whatever their accent might be.

While teachers of younger children will be familiar with this business of phoneme-grapheme correspondence in their teaching of reading, colleagues working with older children may not be. Yet this correspondence helps us to view the reading and writing process through the eyes of older EAL learners who are literate in their first language. The printed words you are reading are made up of letters of the roman alphabet. To get meaning out of the words you have to process them in a number of ways, one of which is to match the letters to sounds of words. You are reading an English text so you use the letters to generate English words and you do this by drawing on your knowledge of phoneme-grapheme correspondence in English to match sound values to the letters – sometimes one letter to one sound, and sometimes two or more letters to one sound. But the roman alphabet is used by many other languages, each with its own system of phoneme-grapheme correspondence. EAL pupils who first learned to read in another language that uses the roman alphabet, say Turkish or Czech, have to adjust their knowledge of L_1 phoneme-grapheme correspondence to accommodate the way English operates. This can be achieved fairly rapidly by EAL pupils who are confidently literate in L_1: they have already learned the complex processing of print and thus acquired a highly automated set of skills. Adding an alternative set of phoneme-grapheme 'matches' is a relatively mechanical task. Adult native-speakers of English who disclaim knowledge of another language still know how to 'decode' by matching phonemes to graphemes in ways that are different from their L_1:

> Ciao
> Au revoir
> Hasta mañana.

Learning to read involves a good deal more than decoding. Having worked out the symbol-sound matches of say, the Cyrillic alphabet, you still need to understand the messages of words and sentences you are able to 'sound out'. Reading for comprehension brings us full circle, back to our concern with lexical meaning in English. Current debate about the teaching of reading is highlighting the advantages of teaching 'phonics' i.e. phoneme-grapheme correspondence. One thing the debate disregards (largely because it is a debate which has been hijacked by political prescriptivism) is whether teachers maintain a meaning-seeking approach to texts. Many children who become adept at handling the complexities of English orthography are masking their lack of comprehension of the words and phrases they read.

Many languages (Russian, Hindi, Spanish, for example) have a high level of regularity in phoneme-grapheme correspondence because they have, at difference points in their history, been 'reformed'. British English has resisted such reforms and so many spellings present problems in reading and writing – for both native and EAL learners. The essential approach to tackling reading is to combine decoding skills with meaning-seeking skills.

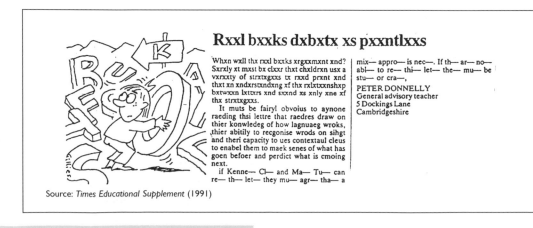

Rxxl bxxks dxbxtx xs pxxntlxxs

Whxn wxll thx rxxl bxxks xrgxxmxnt xnd? Sxrxly xt mxst bx clxxr thxt chxldrxn usx a vxrxxty of strxtxgxxs tx rxxd prxnt xnd thxt xn xndxrstxndxng xf thx rxlxtxxnshxp bxtwxxn lxttxrs xnd sxxnd xs xnly xne xf thx strxtxgxxs.

It muts be fairyl obvoius to aynone raeding thsi lettre that raedres draw on thier konwledeg of how lagnuaeg wroks, thier abitily to recgonise wrods on sihgt and theri capacity to ues contextaul cleus to enabel them to maek senes of what has goen befoer and perdict what is cmoing next.

if Kenne— Cl— and Ma— Tu— can re— th— let— they mu— agr— tha— a

mix— appro— is nec—. If th— ar— no— abl— to re— thi— let— the— mu— be stu— or cra—,

PETER DONNELLY
General advisory teacher
5 Dockings Lane
Cambridgeshire

Source: *Times Educational Supplement* (1991)

Homophones and **homographs** of English warrant particular attention by EAL learners, preferably as they occur in curriculum texts, to ensure that their meanings are related to the topic. You might, however, use the poem below with colleagues and older learners to discuss the problems caused by English orthography. Note how the vowel sounds are the main culprits, and ask pupils to explain how vowels operate in other languages. In syllabic writing systems such as Urdu and Hindi and other South Asian languages use, vowel sounds are represented by **diacritics** – accents and dots. Older EAL learners who are literate in these languages benefit from understanding the correspondence of L_1 and English vowel representation. Teachers who share these (and other) languages with their pupils can turn this activity into great advantage as a regular device for pointing out the orthographic behaviour of English and its comparison with L_1. And for English mother-tongue pupils these activities explain the fundamentals of orthography which give them insights into the way languages of the world operate.

English Pronunciation

I take it you already know
Of tough and bough and cough and dough?
Others may stumble but not you,
On hiccough, thorough, laugh and through.
Well done! And now you wish, perhaps,
To learn of less familiar traps?

Beware of heard, a dreadful word
That looks like beard and sounds like bird,
And dead: it's said like bed, not bead –
For goodness sake don't call it 'deed'!
Watch out for meat and great and threat
(They rhyme with suite and straight and debt).

A moth is not a moth in mother
Nor both in bother, broth in brother,
And here is not a match for there
Nor dear and fear for bear and pear,
Just look them up – and goose and choose,
And cork and work and card and ward,
And font and front and word and sword,
And do and go and thwart and cart –
Come, come, I've hardly made a start!
A dreadful language? Snakes alive!
I'd mastered it when I was five.

TSW (initials only given, from a letter in the *Sunday Times*, 3 Jan, 1965 (cited in Mackay and Thompson, 1968).

Cultural fun

We've seen that attention to the constituent parts of a text, i.e. the lexical units (words and phrases) is as important as understanding and responding to the whole message of a text. Texts, of course, are not all purely verbal. They come in many forms – as stories spoken and written, as pieces of information, jokes, photographs, charts, performances and so on. We 'read' texts with cultural eyes and ears, and the more we are 'tuned in' culturally, the more we are linguistically enabled by the form of the text, irrespective of whether we agree with or like the message of the text.

Many **jokes** provide short texts which rely on cultural knowledge as well as multiple word meaning and sound similarity. Chiario (1992) talks of jokes as cultural ritual 'identifiable by the frame around which they are constructed':

– Why did the bees go on strike?
They wanted more honey and shorter flowers.

With help from our pupils we can find ways to make English joke frames culturally inclusive:

– Why did the Bangra dancer fall over after his breakfast?
Because he had scrambled legs.

– Knock knock
Who's there?
Amir
Amir who?
I'm still 'ere.

When a text is culturally dense the lexical units are likely to demand a high level of attention for the whole message to be appreciated. The following text provides us with an experience of reading which demands a good deal of concentration on lexical form as well as cultural content. The reading task we face here gives an idea of the demands on EAL learners whose knowledge of English is limited by cultural gaps (see opposite).

In texts like this, paraphrase and summary destroy the richly layered images which make the text worth reading. In order to access these images we must engage closely with the words and phrases as they are assembled by the author. We must also bring to the reading task a sustained attitude of meaning-seeking so that, item by item, the detailed scenario is revealed and we are 'in the picture'.

There are good reasons to work with older EAL learners on texts which are dense in cultural connotation and figurative meaning as 'foreign language' passages which need to be investigated in some of the traditions of 'foreign language' translation. Instead of simplifying them we can approach them as

A proposal of marriage (Nidderdale, 1866)

My dere miss,

I now take hup my pen tow rite yow opin fulines will find yow well as it leaves me at present – thank God for it. You will praps be supprised that i should maik soa bolde as tow rite to yow who is sutch a ladi and i hop that yow will not bee vexd at mee for it. I hardly dare say wat i want i ham so timid about ladis and mi and trimmels like a hespin lefe. I once seed in a book that faint art nevver won fare ladi so here goaz.

I am a farmar in a smal wai and mi age is rayther more that 40 yere and mi mother lives with me and keeps my house and shee as been very powerly laitly and cannot stur about mutch and i think i shud be more comfurtabler with a wife. I have had mi hi on yow a long time and i think that yow are a very nice young wumman and one that wud mak me appi iff onley yow think soa. We keep a survant girl to milk 3 kye and dow the work in the ouse and she goes out a bit in the sumer to gadder wickins and shee snags a fu of turnips in the backhend and we keep a gai strang lad to go with the draft and setterha. I dow a good piece of work on the farm miself and attends paitley market and i sum times show a fu of sheep and i feeds between 3 and 4 pigs againe cristmas and the same is very youseful in th ouse to maik pize and keakes and soaforth and i sels the hams to elp to pai for the barley meal.

I ave about 73 pund in naisbro bank and we ave a nice little parlor down stares with a blu carpet and a huven on one side ov the fire-plaice and the old wumman on th uther side smoking. The golden rules claimed up on the wals abuv the long settle and you cud sit awl the day in the ezy chare and nit and mend my kytles and leggums and you cud maik the t readdy again i cum in and you cud make the butter for paitley market and i wud drive you to church every sunday in the spring cart and i would dowall that lays in my power to make you happy. So i hop to hear from you as i am in desprit ard yurnist and wil marrie you at mai day or if my mother dees afore Ise want you afore if only you wil exep of me. And mi dere we cud be verri appi togedder and i oap yow will let me now your mind by retern of poast and iff you are faverable i wil cum up to the scratch soa noa moor at preasent from your wel wisher and tru luvve....

Pea hes – i hop yow wil sai nothing about this if you wil not excep of me as i have anuther very nice wumman in mi hi and i think i shall marrie her if you do not excepp of me but i thrught yow wud suite mi muther better- the same venerable speciman of the feamale biped (excuse me but this is owr skule master's remark and hes a clever man) being very crusty at times so i tell you before you cum she will be maister.

Source: *The Dalesman*

problem-solving activities and apply knowledge of lexical behaviours to access the meanings, using the overhead projector for whole-class reading. Dictionaries – both English-English and bilingual – and thesauri may be used to tackle the lexical items which are identified as problematic.

Let's continue to enjoy the 'howlers' that occur as children are learning the word-meaning/culture game but let's turn 'howlers' into 'how to' teach cultural meaning:

– What should you be careful of during windy weather?
Falling trees – you could be captivated.

– From what might men suffer in their fifties?
The manopause.

– What was Einstein's theory of relativity?
A sort of family tree that only he could understand.

– What is the meaning of the word *effluent*?
Effluent is the word you can't be if you want your dole money.

– What is the function of antibodies?
Antibodies are organisations in dispute with people.

Source: *Daily Mirror, Yes! Magazine* 1994

Notes and References

1   With thanks to Graham Williamson for this example.

2   Thankyou Barré Fitzpatrick for this comment.

3   Thankyou Barry Miller for this item!

4   Thanks, Trees!

5   There are many sources of detailed information about orthography and about individual languages. For a brief general overview see Crystal, 1987.

Chapter Five

Words to work on

Word-meaning exploration needs its own place on the time-table – at all Key Stages of the school curriculum. As well as attending to lexical items in curriculum activities and subject lessons, EAL learners benefit from focusing on lexical items as a study in their own right. Words, as we have seen, need a context in order to convey meaning, but we can nevertheless examine them in ways that promote the attitude of meaning-seeking which children must carry from one subject context to another. This chapter returns to the framework of lexical behaviours to propose activities and resources for using as short 'spotlight' sessions, or combined in more extended project approaches to word meaning-seeking.

Schools that provide well for EAL learners are those where linguistic meaning *per se* is consistently high in teacher consciousness in all areas of the curriculum, and where a coordinated policy ensures that time is regularly allocated to the study of meaning. Abundant evidence demonstrates that attention to the *forms* of language as well as to messages is a significant factor in the achievement of additional language learners. If you refer back to the contrived French rhyme in Chapter One, you will remember how, when you 'got the message' – that is, recognised the whole text for what it was – you (probably) paid little more attention to the lexical units that the text contained – at least, not enough to remember those lexical items now! When we 'simplify' demanding texts for EAL learners or summarise long texts for them, we help them gain access to the messages of the text at the expense of attending to the forms of the texts. The cumulative effect of this kind of 'help' is that the EAL learners come not to expect to apply mental energy to the many words and phrases which carry the meanings in text. This is *not* laziness but confusion or disengagement, which grows from lack of awareness about the importance of attending to the forms of meaning in words and phrases.

Mercer (in Mercer and Swann, 1996) talks about the reluctance of children to 'show their ignorance' of subject terminology:

A consequence may be that many technical words become for children mere jargon, words which they know they are expected to use but which mean very little to them.

Educational research has provided many bizarre and salutary examples of how technical English terms may be misunderstood and most teachers will have their own collections. Two examples I have recorded are those of a 12-year-old who thought that 'quandary' meant a four-sided figure and a 16-year-old who, after saying that he never understood 'subtractions', later commented that he could do 'take-aways'. Robert Hull, a British secondary teacher has noted these kind of problems among 14-year-old pupils:

'Animals harbour insects' means they ate them. The 'lowest bridge-town' was a slum on a bridge... Expressions such as 'molten iron', 'physical feature', 'factor', 'western leader' were often insuperable obstacles to comprehension' [Hull, R. 1985 The Language Gap London: Methuen]. (Mercer and Swann, 1996)

Spotlight sessions

By giving time to the study of lexical behaviours (polysemy, collocation etc.) we promote shared consciousness of the need to attend to the bits and pieces of speech and written texts. The ideal approach to 'spotlighting' is a coordinated plan that links subject areas, whether they be topics in the primary school or different timetabled subjects at secondary level. For example, in Key Stage planning, the target words and phrases of different topic/subject areas (or NC programmes of Study) can be identified as needing 'spotlight sessions'. These could be part of a primary teacher's planning for one class, or agreed between secondary subject teachers led by the English (as a subject) teacher. So, for example, a session on similes will include examples from science (as solid as a rock, as heavy as lead), from geography (as old as the hills, as dry as dust) etc. A session on metaphors and idioms will take words and phrases from Maths (square, set, angle, line) and from PE (the ball's in your court, keep your eye on the ball, cross the line) etc. Using Jim Cummins' (1996) guidelines (see page 147), we should avoid choosing words and phrases randomly for study and instead alert children to the connections between lexical behaviour and ideas which have priority in their crowded curriculum. Not that we should under-estimate children's capacity to learn and enjoy the patterns that lexical behaviours form. In looking at phrasal verbs, for example (see page 149), we can get them to see that frequently-occurring English verbs use particles (about, above, before, in, off, up etc.) in predictable meanings. Children will also have many ideas of their own from L_1 and English and we really want to create an ethos which encourages them to turn the 'spotlight' onto words and phrases which intrigue them or puzzle them.

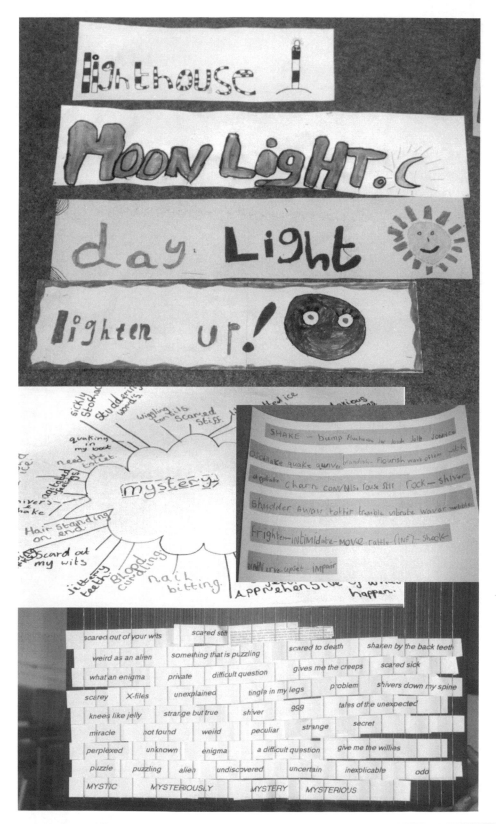

With thanks to teachers participating in the
in-service course 'Word-Weaving' 1996

With thanks to teachers participating in the in-service course 'Word-Weaving' 1996

Just as children can be taught to understand the concept of 'verbs' and 'adjectives', they can be taught the ideas of 'polysemy', 'collocation', 'metaphor', 'antonyms' etc. My experience is that teachers are repeatedly surprised and impressed at children's eagerness to explore these ideas and contribute their own examples of word behaviours. Even very young children enjoy playing with the rhythm and rhyme of words, visual jokes that can be made out of figurative expressions, dance and movement to interpret different verbs of movement like *twist* and *twirl, shake* and *shiver, wave* and *waggle*. The teacher, as model meaning-seeker, is the most powerful influence on children's engagement with words and creating an ethos which combines enjoyment with stimulating semantic curiosity.

In primary schools where children have a classroom base, there are quick, cheap and lively ways to make words and their meanings visible and engaging. If, as in many secondary schools, rooms are allocated to different subject areas, there are opportunities to display words and use standard devices such as the blackboard, overhead projector, logbooks etc. The ideas and resources presented here are not separated by primary and secondary interests because most are adaptable to differing phases and ability groups. Using an overhead projector, for example, is a great way to hold children's attention, especially when they get turns to use it themselves. Story books written for small children can be analysed by teenagers in ways which respect their maturity while helping them understand narrative structure.

Dictionaries and Thesauri

Dictionaries and thesauri – or their equivalents – provide us with immense opportunities to develop language study. Spelling patterns; word families; loan words from all over the globe; changes in definition between old and modern editions; how contexts alter meaning; criteria used by compilers on the inclusion of new words; differences between definitions in several translations; differences determined by the different linguistic levels of several dictionaries from pocket-sized to multi-volume; and many other avenues, can all be explored by pupils, individually or in groups. The compiling of their own dictionaries, using databases, survey results and justifications for inclusion and exclusion of words, is also a worthwhile project. Not least of its likely results is close study of how to construct word definitions, and how to classify words according to root, part of speech, and so on. (THINKLINC Newsletter no. 4. Spring 1991)

Yes, but which dictionaries? Which thesauri? My answer to this question is usually 'lot's of different ones – but especially BIG ones!' I have particular favourites, for reasons I give below:

Longman **Language Activator**

Longman **Dictionary Of Contemporary English**

Collins **Ringbinder Thesaurus**

Oxford **Children's Thesaurus**

Oxford **Children's Dictionary**

Lexicography is a fast-moving science. Advances in the use of computerised data banks have made dictionary compilation vastly more versatile in recent years. One of the biggest changes in English dictionary design has been the **concordance** programs that identify the natural patterns of word usage by native speakers and writers. Sinclair (1987) provides an illustration (see opposite).

This illustrates the meaning potential of a word in varying contexts. As concordance programs are able to draw from tens of millions of spoken and written utterances, the data bank can show which meanings are most frequently used. This gives EAL learners a valuable set of patterns which model native speaker usage, including polysemous uses (literal and figurative). The Longman **Language Activator** and the Longman **Dictionary Of Contemporary English**, though differently organised, both work on this principle of meaning potential.

This recent semantic orientation in EFL is biased towards adult learners and so assumes the learner's cognitive and cultural maturity in L_1:

> When you encode a message, your capacity for applying different linguistic options (associated with delicately different meanings) to one and the same situation derives ultimately from the fact that we human beings are blessed with a gift of making sense of a situation in a number of different, and sometimes even divergent ways. For example, we can say that someone 'snuffed it' if we want to be rather callous or humorous about someone dying, as well as using 'pass away' if we are trying to be sensitive and refer only obliquely to a friend's relative dying. It will not be difficult to see that something like this is involved in all kinds of 'rhetorical' use of language, as in exaggeration, humour, irony, euphemism, and metaphor. (Ikegami, Y in Summers et al. 1993:F20)

Although both dictionaries are aimed at older users, they have been used with splendid results by teachers with young EAL learners – even in nursery classes. Young children are fascinated by 'big books', and when their teacher exudes personal enthusiasm they become infected with curiosity about the words and how they are organised. Even, indeed especially at early stages of literacy and EAL acquisition, there should be an expectation of meaning-seeking, which will be vital to the learner throughout their learning. **Dictionary-dipping** is an

Concordance Extract from the Main Corpus for 'mind'

```
GW0034 BR BR  ay inhibit the formation of an original idea in a mind capable of original ideas. It may be better t
GW0086 BR BR  the first chance!" But Mr. Evans in his tormented mind cared nothing whether John liked the tower or
GW0033 BR BR  er bother with more? Why even mention love, never mind carry on about how love itself must evolve to
GW0086 BR BR  e the little urchin again." And then Tom Barter's mind ceased suddenly to think in definite words. T
GW0086 BR BR  as if they were perfectly meaningless sounds, his mind ceased to bed. He felt the pressure of her br
GW0002 BR BR  ?' "I suppose he left it in the safe.' "Would you mind checking up? "I'll ask his secretary--oh, I'
GW0052 BR BR  JACWA, in developing their plans, had to bear in mind certain considerations arising from the new c
GW0081 BR BR  who are impelled by their own inner needs, often mind children when the job is really beyond their
GW0071 AM BR  lasses and she paid for her own meals. She didn't mind cigarette smoke any more. She had no lovers.
GW0012 BR BR  all museums for the curious Londoner, making the mind clang with astonishment— consid? er the neol
GW0076 BR BR  ffering from anaemia. When this was rectified her mind cleared and she was able to return to normal I
GW0075 BR BR  public readings; and the worry in the back of his mind clouds the understanding he is fighting for a
GW0072 AM BR  irt and scanties? Did I have something special in mind? coaxing voices asked me. Swimming suits? We
GW0078 OT BR  s, however improbable such a creature may be. The mind comprehends facts and is at ease with fiction
GW0078 OT BR  nded on from generation to generation. The modern mind, conditioned as it is to the devouring needs
GW0086 BR BR  . Geard; but I'm a black sheep, you know. I don't mind confessing to all you kind people "—here he
GW0072 AM BR  meals snacks, outdoor barbecues – but which in my mind conjured up odious visions of stinking high s
GW0032 AM BR  just live with this and not fight it mentally ... mind control... I should talk now about Phaedrus'
GW0032 AM BR  is idea that the entire world is within one's own mind could be dismissed as absurd if Hume had just
GW0034 BR BR  go I became interested in finding out whether the mind could experience a visual hallucination which
GW0034 BR BR  thetic mysticism, but an inquiry into whether the mind could hold vividly in consciousness an experi
GW0055 AM BR  been burned with the hot iron. He found that his mind could focus better now on the only choice tha
GW0072 AM BR  t her mouth to my ear -- but for quite a while my mind could not separate into words the hot thunder
GS0022        stion that what may be partly in the questioners mind could be answered by reference to language p
GW0117 OT BR  .'" Occur where?' " enquired Mr. Dekker. "In the mind!" could jubilantly soar on the wings of that su
GW0086 BR BR  .'" Occur where? " enquired Mr. Dekker. "In the mind," cried the Welshman, raising his hand to his
GW0019 AU BR  eth. I got away from the gate for a second and my mind crystallized. I raced for some ropes, a wood
GW0055 AM BR  ace t0 which, for no explicable reason your adult mind darts back when you Mine is a weatherbeaten,
GW0058 AM BR  elf with his chin against his clasped knees, his mind dazed and reeling with all that he had seen a
GW0068 AA     ics. She had tried to educate herself gently, her mind dazed by even the simplest terms, and had in
GW0001 AM BR  d of that rocky day, and hear her saying, "Never mind, dear, you can't win 'em all.' And he says,"
GW0031 AM BR  ed circle of ce.ebrityhood, and old images in the mind decay to make way for the new. The some might
GW0073 BR BR  which had disintegrated. Moreover, some habits of mind derived from it, notably traditional habitat
GW0004 BR BR  ut.Man, being dexterous of hand and inventive of mind, did neither. H e hunted the furred animals,
GI0086 BR BR  andie!' thought Mr. Evans, The Welshman's triadic mind dived like a plummet, then, to the sea- botto
GW0034 BR BR  ore difficult to change the parts themselves. The mind divides the continuity of the world around us
GW0052 BR BR  s waiting for the blow to fall. <p 24> "You don't mind, do you.' Sarah asked, "if it's a cold meal t
GS0127 BR BR  urely? ((B)) I don't mind ((C)) Would Nick really mind, do you think? ((B)) Erm. No, I shouldn't thi
GW0019 BR BR  But I just feel so happy in this house. You don't mind do you? "I'm not sure it's a wildly good id
GS0039        ng the right rituals at the right times. I don't mind doing those things I thing the trouble is t
GW0119 BR BR  ys Howard, "we'd better rush. "Howard, would you mind down to the exigencies of survival, he is free
GW0078 OT BR  ng no excuse for the anxieties which drag a man's mind drifted off Lamin 'to other things. He thought
GW0055 AM BR  left the children and the village behind, Kunta's mind drinking alone.' "He said if I didn't pull up
GW0052 BR BR  octors always do, don't they?' <P 165> "I don't mind driving a little way along and seeing if they
GW0019 AU BR  p and stopped. I asked them if they <P 146> would mind drugs, drink, everything. He hates universit
GW0143 BR BR  interesting type,' he said. "Rick nearly blew his mind, during my daymares and insomnias. More pre- c
GW0072 AM BR  aw her constantly and obsessively in my conscious mind during pillow-talk; his preoccupation with th
GW0080 BR BR  fficially George's idea, doubtless planted in his mind emotional make-up and body on the one hand a
GW0078 BR BR  ma? de between what a man is given in the way of mind, emotion and senses maintain their hold on re
GW0078 OT BR  and rejection of the partial images through which mind, engaged with them, I can see a sort of intell
GS0098        eresting. I can remember things when I can get my mind er, er George Bernard Shaw, the English have no
GS0157 BR BR  t's the extent of your world and also bearing in mind even as I had left the Strykers' cabin. If sh
GW0031 AM BR  ich this pessimis-tic prophecy grips the popular mind, even now when I know what to seek in the past
GW0026 BR BR  r any of the questions that had half-formed in my mind
GW0072 AM BR  ntation? than they present themselves with to my mind
```

Source: Sinclair (1987) *Looking Up: an account of the COBUILD Project in lexical computing*.

Longman Contemporary English Dictionary (1993).
Reprinted by permission of Addison Wesley-Longman Ltd.

endless means of exploring word-meaning. It can easily be fitted into registration time and between activities or combined with learning alphabetical order.

Concordance choices (meaning 1, meaning 2 etc. on the basis of frequency) are not always what is needed in a curriculum context where words are used in academic ways. Sometimes less common, even somewhat dated terms are needed, and other types of dictionaries will be more useful.

That children are willing to persist with adult dictionaries organised for EAL learners has been observed by teachers across age-ranges. But children do become frustrated if they have to struggle with alphabetical ordering and page numbering, only to find that the word they want is not included. This can happen with small, limited entry dictionaries but well designed dictionaries and thesauri for children offer clearer typography, fewer abbreviations and acronyms, and entries relevant to different age-ranges.

The Oxford *Children's Dictionary*, for example includes:

bike	laptop
byte	minaret (picture)
disc	noodles
dishwasher	Ramadan
Diwali	salaam
duvet	sari (picture)
keyboard	

The important thing to convey to children is that dictionaries are powerful tools-of-trade in language acquisition. A school's book collection must include bilingual dictionaries for each home language spoken, and these must not be left to gather dust on the shelf in the staff-room! Bilingual dictionaries, too, will vary in quality and suitability for different purposes. Bilingual adults are not automatically skilled dictionary users and translators, and may need time to develop such skills. By working on the ideas of lexical behaviour in this book, colleagues of different language repertoires will be able to identify the best ways to use dictionaries and thesauri.

Spotlight on...

The 'Spotlight' ideas in this chapter are grouped under headings of lexical behaviours highlighted throughout earlier chapters. Some of these activities might seem to be from a bygone age when grammar exercises (the 'real work') in English textbooks were interspersed with snippets of word-play, or collections of homonyms, opposites and the like, ostensibly for light relief. Have we perhaps thrown out the baby with the bath water by ignoring the value of 'de-contextualised' vocabulary exercises? It takes a while to get into the habit of noticing examples of homonyms or similes or whatever, and a good way to get started is to dip into collections in publications dedicated to exploring the rich diversity of lexical meaning in English and other languages. The source books referred to in this chapter are all for the English language and provide a wealth of classroom-friendly ideas which, with preparation and use of dictionaries, can become bilingual activities. So, for example, turning the spotlight on figurative expressions provides opportunities for some lively cross-lingual meaning-seeking for all children.

Children can involve their families in researching L$_1$ and additional language equivalents

HAIR-RAISING →	← KEEP YOUR HEAD ABOVE WATER
MY EARS ARE BURNING →	← ONE IN THE EYE FOR
POKE YOUR NOSE IN →	← PAIN IN THE NECK
ARMED TO THE TEETH →	← CHIN UP
A MILLSTONE ROUND MY NECK →	← STICK YOU NECK OUT
SPIT IT OUT →	← HARD TO SWALLOW
THICK-SKINNED →	← TAKE IT TO HEART
THE HEART OF THE MATTER →	← MUSCLE IN
ELBOW GREASE →	← GET IT OFF YOUR CHEST
KNUCKLE DOWN→	← GIVE YOU A HAND
ALL FINGERS AND THUMBS →	← HAVE A BELLYFUL
BUMS ON SEATS →	← TURN YOUR BACK ON SOMEONE
MY KNEES WERE KNOCKING →	← KNEE-HIGH TO A GRASSHOPPER
TWO LEFT FEET →	← GET YOUR SKATES ON
DIP YOUR TOE IN THE WATER →	← ONE FOOT IN THE DOOR

Drawing by Georgia Woollard

The benefits of children using their home language in the classroom are extensively documented (see, for example, Wong-Fillmore and Valdez, 1986, Ellis, 1994; Thomas and Collier, 1995). Cummins (1984) especially has influenced educational thinking, pointing to the enhanced cognitive processing that may accrue from children's application of L_1 to their L_2 learning. He draws attention to 'cognitive, academic linguistic proficiency' which is better developed by drawing on the 'common underlying proficiency' of bilingualism than by relying solely on operating in a weaker L_2. But in the UK the cognitive benefits of operating bilingually have scarcely affected policy. The idea of 'valuing' children's home languages, though vital for children's sense of well-being, does not provide strategic pedagogic approaches to developing academic linguistic proficiency – strategies which alert children to the power of words in shaping their futures. Cummins (1996) reminds us of the huge problem facing EAL learners who are given no extra time to 'catch up' with their English mother-tongue peers while accessing the curriculum through English:

> Effective instruction that will give students access to the power of language and accelerate their academic growth must include the following components:
>
> * active communication of meaning
>
> * cognitive challenge
>
> * contextual support
>
> * building student self-esteem
>
> Cummins (1996)

So, although 'traditional' texts such as *First Aid in English* (MacIver, 1986) might provide ready examples of English collective nouns etc., I would refer you to Jim Cummins' (1996) framework of 'Education for Empowerment' as guidelines for drawing on the ideas and resources suggested in this chapter. Four main principles are proposed by Cummins:

– Activate prior knowledge/Build background knowledge

– Present cognitively engaging input with appropriate contextual supports

– Encourage active language use to connect input with students' prior experience and with thematically-related content

– Assess student learning in order to provide feedback that will build language awareness and efficient learning strategies

Source: Ch 4 'Accelerating Academic Language Learning' in Jim Cummins *Negotiating Identities: Education for Empowerment in a Diverse Society* (CABE; from Trentham Books, 1996).

Turning the spotlight on lexical behaviours is open-ended. I offer examples of lexical behaviours which I hope will trigger others that are relevant to the themes and topics you are pursuing in curriculum contexts and provide ideas for collaboration between teachers, so that children become accustomed to seeking the meaning potential of lexical items in varied contexts. I hope that the resources suggested here will stimulate active, 'imageful' inter-lingual word play and never dull, gap-filling exercises.

So, let's get weaving...

Spotlight on POLYSEMY

'Easy' words that have multiple meaning potential in **collocation,** and **phrasal verbs** can be examined in ways which draw from children's knowledge about language and their own cultural experiences. Give children turns at the blackboard and overhead projector to 'brainstorm' these 'little' words:

SET	TURN
set off	turn the tables
set the table	have a funny turn
game, set and match	turn tail
set in concrete	
SQUARE	MIND
a square peg	do you mind
square meal	would you mind
square deal	mind the gap
back to square one	mind the baby
square your shoulders	mind your own business
	mind how you go
	mind you...

– Look in the **Longman English Contemporary Dictionary** and the **Longman Language Activator** for more multiple meanings of words of high frequency. MATCH THEM TO L_1 LEXICAL ITEMS:

LOOK
CATCH
SAY
HIGH
LOW
FAST
SLOW

Spotlight on PHRASAL VERBS

– Look in the **Cobuild Dictionary of Phrasal Verbs** to match common verbs + particles with more formal 'synonyms':

> turn down = reject, refuse
> get by = manage
> hang on = wait
> build up = increase
> sweep away = destroy
> put in = insert

– Make a large wall display of the **particles** in the **Cobuild Dictionary of Phrasal Verbs** and refer to it when phrasal verbs crop up(!):

aback	around	between	of	through
about	as	beyond	off	to
above	aside	by	on	together
across	at	down	onto	towards
after	away	for	out	under
against	back	forth	over	up
ahead	before	forward	overboard	upon
along	behind	from	past	with
among	below	in	round	without
apart	beneath	into		

source: Collins COBUILD Dictionary of Phrasal Verbs.

Spotlight on COLLOCATION

– Look at the way that words occur together regularly – e.g. *high probability*, but *good* (not *high*) *chance*. Collocation affects the whole meaning of the lexical unit, e.g. *slim chance* and *fat chance* are not opposites.

– Look at how words also collocate in some kinds of text, without necessarily being right next to each other. For example, in a recipe, a sports commentary, a holiday brochure.

– On an advert (photocopied onto paper or overhead transparency), children can ring the words and phrases which collocate to give the text its desired communicative effect.

❑ **New Kodak Royal Gold**

Using Kodak's advanced T-Grain emulsion technology, Royal Gold films offer a stunning combination of clarity, definition, sharpness and colour in a full range of speeds, making them ideal for even the most demanding photographer.

Kodak Royal Gold – Clarity, Sharpness and Definition

– Take a topic like HOUSES and brainstorm the words which 'hang around' each other:

DOOR – handle, knob, latch, sneck, lintel, threshold, architrave, open, close, slam, draught...

WINDOW – pane, curtains, pelmet, view, look out ....

– Paste magazine pictures, related to your topic, in the middle of a large sheet of paper for children to work on in pairs...

Spotlight on WORDS LINKED with *AND*

Words linked with *and* can be put into a table, chopped up on cards, sorted, illustrated.... Give children the task of researching them:

fair and square	flesh and
home and dry	bits and
touch and	hot and
airs and	rise and
sick and	

Collocations like these reinforce cultural conventions. Find out how other languages use words joined with *and* ...

Spotlight on HOMONYMS (homophones and homographs)

Homophones are words which sound the same but have different meanings. Homographs are words which are spelt in the same way but pronounced differently and with different meanings:

beat	⟷ beat		wind	⟷ wind
sale	⟷ sail		lead	⟷ lead
pedal	⟷ peddle		bow	⟷ bow

– Ask pupils for *homonyms in different languages and across languages*

Words which sound similar, and are easily misheard (taxes ⟷ taxis) are the stuff of Knock Knock jokes.

– Make a *joke dip*

– On computer – a *knock knock* data base

– Hang up your homonyms on a *word-tree*

– Collect words which sound like same (or similar) across different languages.

Spotlight on COMPOUND WORDS

– Collect compound words as they occur in topics and look at their meaning potential

e.g.
BED
bedrock
flowerbed

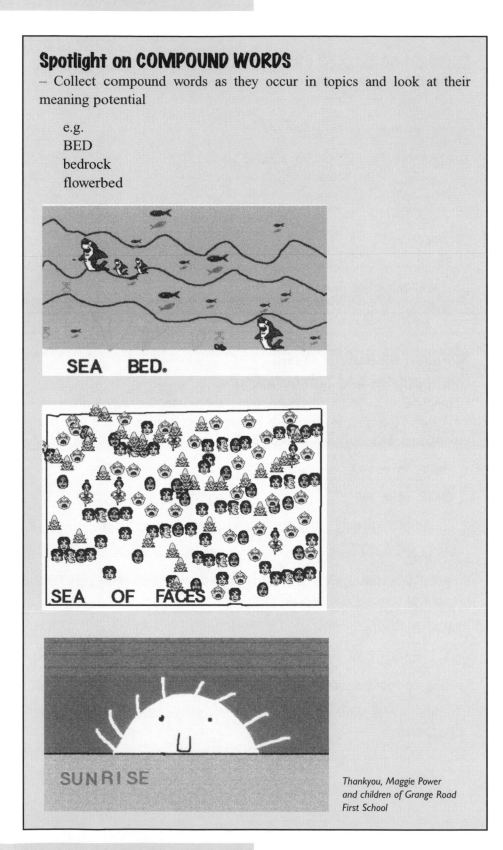

Thankyou, Maggie Power
and children of Grange Road
First School

Spotlight on LITERAL/FIGURATIVE DISTINCTIONS in polysemous words

denotation

Even texts which strive for a plain, unambiguous meaning contain words which have multiple meanings:

'DO NOT OPEN INBOARD FAN COWL UNTIL LEADING EDGE SLATS ARE RETRACTED AND DEACTIVATED.

SEE INSTRUCTIONS INSIDE OUTBOARD DOOR'

(Seen on the engine housing of a LOT aeroplane.)

IMPORTANT NOTICE
THIS WALK IS STRENUOUS & IN PARTS DANGEROUS KEEP TO THE MAIN PATH. KEEP CHILDREN UNDER CONTROL STRONG BOOTS OR SHOES SHOULD BE WORN

– Look into words that have both kinds of meaning – literal and figurative:

NET in *casting the net*

SAIL in *sailing close to the wind*

SALT in *salt of the earth*

FLOAT in *floating the idea*

OAR in *putting an oar in*

– Ask children to 'image' the maritime influence in these and other English expressions. Can you think of sets from sport, from cooking... What equivalents are there in e.g. Urdu, French, Polish, Caribbean Creoles? Who in your family will know?

Spotlight on SYNONYMS and ANTONYMS

Is there such a thing as synonym?

– Look into the difference of effect in closely matched pairs of words:

hard
which meaning?

hard, not soft	➜ •HARD
difficult	➜ •DIFFICULT
making you very tired	➜ •TIRED
strict, severe	➜ •STRICT
cruel to other people	➜ •CRUEL

• HARD

1. words for describing something that does not change its shape when you press down on it

    HARD
    SOLID
    FIRM

2. words that describe something that is difficult or impossible to bend

    HARD
    STIFF
    RIGID

3. words for describing food that is difficult or impossible to cut or eat

    HARD
    TOUGH

4. words for describing skin or material that is very hard

    HARD
    LEATHERY

5. to become hard

    HARDEN
    SET
    SOLIDIFY
    FREEZE

6. to make something harder

    HARDEN
    STIFFEN

Source: Longman Language Activator

Spotlight on SYNONYMS and ANTONYMS (continued)

– Dip into the *Dictionary of Synonyms and Antonyms* by Laurence Urdang (Macmillan 1995)

Command of word meaning involves being able to differentiate meanings.

– Follow up a storybook with chart-making.

SIX DINNER SID by Inga Moore (1990) is one of my favourites

fur	scratch
wool	stroke
hair	tickle
coat	rub
pelt	caress

Sometimes we can use these interchangeably, sometimes it's important to apply them differentially.

– Act out *squash/squeeze/press; lean/bend/turn; queasy/dizzy/weary*

Spotlight on GRADATION and SCALE

With thanks to teachers participating in the
in-service course 'Word-Weaving' 1996

Spotlight on SIMILES

They're formulaic, they're explicit, but they're culturally dense. Learners need to explore the cultural ideas behind them and match them with L_1 similes. They need to recognise the forms of similes, be encouraged to find them in speech and written texts, and to use them for their own purposes. Equivalent similes in other languages will bring fresh insight to clichéd English similes.

– as dry as a bone	– like a red rag to a bull
– as cool as a cucumber	– like a bull in a china shop
– as clear as mud	– like taking candy from a baby
– as drunk as a lord	– like a bolt from the blue
– as fit as a fiddle	– like water off a duck's back
– as round as a barrel	– like a right lemon
– as steady as a rock	– like a fish out of water
– quick as a flash	

– A **simile snake** can wind its way around the classroom wall, under and over desks and across the ceiling.

Showing respect for children's maturity is crucial for the morale of older learners. Choose the very common similes that English native speakers use unconsciously. But don't regard this and other ideas as only suited to young children – you can get older learners into similes by giving them the design task of producing a **simile snake** for children in a younger class; or set it up as a computer game, guessing the last half of the simile; or make the similes memorable through drama, mime and artwork. But beware: don't allow learners to fill their time using glue and scissors without attending to the similes.

The Guinness Book of Words by Martin Manser (1988) has a good collection of similes, with explanations of their derivation:

> As sure as eggs is eggs. This expression, used to mean 'definitely' or 'certainly', is an alteration of the 17th century mathematical statement 'as sure as x is x'.

Your pupils may like to research the historical origins these or improvise / write / illustrate their own fanciful stories of origin.

Spotlight on CLICHÉS and CATCH PHRASES

EAL learners may or may not interact with English native speakers. So not all have the opportunities to acquire some of the thousands of formulas that make up everyday speech and that they need to understand and speak, if they are to avoid sounding stiff and formal. They must learn that catch phrases can be inappropriate in certain formal contexts and writing. **Matching the clichés with synonymous expressions** of a more formal style will give them useful options:

– be that as it may	– it goes to show you never can tell
– not a blind bit of notice	– wouldn't say boo to a goose
– nice weather for ducks	– wouldn't hurt a fly
– don't push your luck	– can't see the wood for the trees
– what is the world coming to?	– it's daylight robbery
– it frightened the living daylights out of me	

Find catch-phrases that come from story

jack rabbit
sleeping beauty
feeding of the five thousand
and refrains
I'll huff and I'll puff...

also from nursery rhymes, poetry and drama and songs...

Clichés can pile up for varying effect. Have another look at the 'Housework' scenario on p 27. Notice that the speaker doesn't actually tell us what happened in any literal sense, but we get a good idea of what was going on from the expressions used.

– Print out a **Cliché collection** on slips of paper. Pupils can use these to write short scenarios, for example:

– finding something that was lost	(needle in a haystack; turned the room upside down)
– somebody telling a lie	(butter wouldn't melt in his mouth; all come out in the wash)
– a difficult journey	All around the houses; come hell or high water)
– a pleasant surprise	(out of the blue; couldn't believe my eyes)

Spotlight on ARCHAISMS

Many idioms are archaic, remnants of **sea-faring/rural culture,** for example. Other languages will match the deep semantic meaning with expressions drawn from different traditions. Explore across languages to stimulate children's awareness of **semantic equivalents** rather than literal translations:

Sea-faring	Rural trades
Batten down the hatches	hammer and tongs
give a wide berth	irons in the fire
take the wind out of someone's sails	fly off the handle
clear the decks	strike while the iron's hot
high and dry	make hay while the sun shines
between the devil and the deep blue sea	a millstone round your neck
rock the boat	grist to the mill
plain sailing	run of the mill
pull your weight	don't count your chickens
hand over fist	a bird in the hand
sail close to the wind	birds of a feather...

References

– *Dictionary of Clichés* by Christine Ammer (Methuen 1992)

– *Dictionary of English Colloquial Idioms* by F.T.Wood and R.J.Hall (Macmillan 1979)

– *Dictionary of Idioms And Their Origins* by Linda and Roger Flavell (Kyle Cathie 1992)

– One of the best attention-catching devices is a line stretched across a classroom with washing-pegs holding up children's writing. String up a **cliché clothes-line** above the children's heads.

Spotlight on FIGURATIVE MEANINGS

– Look at figurative meaning in idioms, clichés and formulaic expressions
and **image** a literal interpretation of each phrase:

– in the nick of time	– soldier on
– it's just dawned on me	– beaver away
– I've just twigged	– champing at the bit
– on the other hand	– going round in circles
– by the skin of my teeth	– it's the last straw...
– keep your chin up	– don't let the cat out of the bag

Happy (figurative) Families

EGG
egg-head
sure as eggs is eggs
teaching your grandmother to suck eggs
putting your eggs all in one basket
ending up with egg on your face.

SKY

stars in your eyes
every cloud has a silver lining
on the horizon
it dawned on me
in the wind

Now try HORSE and FEET

Spotlight on EUPHEMISM and HYPERBOLE

that is... playing it down or bulling it up...

up at the crack of dawn
on my last legs
a bit of a lad

− *Euphemisms* by John Ayto (Bloomsbury 1994) provides a highly entertaining source of ideas − more suitable for the top end of school age-range and adults.

Spotlight on PROVERBS and HOMILIES

Grandparents are a great source of these and often reflect a community's religious and moral outlook. Homework can elicit refreshing and thought-provoking equivalents in different languages.

– Children can **interview older people** to find out their views on the origins and meanings of:

> – the early bird catches the worm
> – let sleeping dogs lie
> – look before you leap
> – people in glass houses...
> – you can't make an omelette without breaking eggs
> – a bird in the hand...
> – you can take a horse to water...
> – once bitten, twice shy

– Children can discuss their understandings of idioms, figurative expressions, proverbs etc. by imaging in pairs to check that they are 'on the right lines'

References

– Proverbs from *Around the World* by Norma Gleason (Macmillan 1992)

– *Dictionary of Word And Phrase Origins* by Martin Manser (Sphere 1990)

– *English Proverbs Explained* by Ronald Ridout and Clifford Witting (Macmillan 1995)

– *Dictionary of Proverbs and their Origins* by Linda and Roger Flavell (Kyle Cathie 1993)

– *Concise Dictionary of Phrase and Fable* edited by Betty Kirkpatrick (ed) (Helicon Publishing 1993)

Spotlight on CATEGORIZATION

Children need to develop their understanding and use of categorisation in increasingly sophisticated ways. *Yellow Pages* and newspaper advert headings work well with older children. Use the blackboard to start off groupwork on WORD SETS. For example, use a heading (superordinate) like ANIMALS to find a hierarchy of categories -> mammals, fish, birds, insects. Then use each of these to find sets of hyponyms e.g. sparrow, blackbird, gull, robin etc. Choose examples relevant to the topic you are doing. Display the results of the children's findings so it shows that this is on-going work – perhaps a **WORD WALL** that you refer to frequently and the children keep adding to. Let them do the display!

Spotlight on COLLECTIVE NOUNS

– a crowd
– a herd
– a gaggle
– a shoal
– a pride...
– a wobble of jellies
– a dollop of dahl
– a swirl of sarees
– a jangle of bangles

How do collective terms work in other languages?

BIRD GROUPS			
birds in general	flock, flight, volley, congregation, bevy, pod, volary, dissimulation; plump (of wild fowl); brood (of chicks)	mallards	sord, puddling (on water); flush, sute (on land)
		nightingales	match, watch
		owls	stare, parliament
		partridges	covey
bitterns, cranes, herons	sedge, siege	peafowl	muster, pride, ostentation
choughs	chattering, clattering	penguins	rookery, colony
coots	covert, raft	pheasants	nye, bouquet
crows	murder, hover	pigeons	flight, flock
doves	flight, dole, dule, prettying, pitying	plovers	congregation, wing, leash
ducks	flush, team, plump (in flight); dopping (diving); baddling (on water)	quails	bevy, covey
		ravens	unkindness
		rooks	parliament, building, clamour
eagles	convocation		
falcons	cast	snipe	walk, wisp, whisper
finches	trimming, trembling	sparrows	host, quarrel, tribe
geese	gaggle, nide, flock; skein (in flight)	starlings	murmuration
goldfinches, hummingbirds	charm, drum, chattering, troubling	swans	herd, bevy, bank, wedge, game, squadron, whiteness
grouse	covey	teal	spring, raft, coil, knob
gulls	colony		
hawks	cast, leash	thrushes	mutation
jays	band, party	turkeys	flock, dole, dule, raft, raffle, rafter
lapwings	desert, deceit		
		wigeon	company, bunch, knob, coil
larks	exaltation, bevy		
magpies	tittering, tiding	woodcock	fall, covey, plump

Source: *Readers Digest Reverse Dictionary*

Spotlight on DEFINITIONS

Defining words is not easy. Dictionaries use a number of devices and children can try them out:

– according to **function** e.g. it's what you sweep the floor with. My Mum says it's what your bones needs to stay healthy

– giving an **example of type** e.g. a rickshaw is a vehicle, so is a motorbike

– using **opposites** (antonyms), not always straightforward. What's the opposite of *hard*?

– looking at **root-meanings** in multisyllabic words

– by **analogy:** '*it's like...*' or '*it's the same as...*' or, '*you know when you...*'

Spotlight on NAMES and PLACES

Proper nouns which name people – e.g. *Shakil Akhtar* or *Sharon Smith* – may appear to have only one meaning, that is labelling a particular individual. Yet even these labels can be applied to more than one person. I wonder how many Shakil Akhtars and Sharon Smiths there are in UK classrooms?

– Use telephone directories to find common and unusual names

– Looking into the 'meaning' of names in, for example, Brewer's *Dictionary of Names* (Room, 1992), you get a whole new perspective on the 'derived' meanings of people's names. Make sure you find sources which reflect the cultural patterns of your pupils.

– Place names of towns, streets, buildings, contain whole histories:

Shuttleworth Terrace
Brontë Close
Fairweather Green
Centenary Square
Tumbling Hill Street
Kirkgate

Reference

– *Dictionary of Names: people and places and things* by Adrian Room (Helicon Publishing 1993)

Spotlight on DERIVATIONS and BORROWINGS from other languages

Words are part of the complex agreement made by a language community about ways of representing and communicating ideas. Every language community has enough words to express all the ideas it has business with. Very few languages exist in isolation – only in extremely remote geographical situations. Over time, words acquire new meanings, and as communities interact with each other words are borrowed and adapted. (What is the English word for *pizza*?) Words change their meanings through time and every language borrows from others. Good sources for exploring this are:

References

– *Cambridge Encyclopaedia of Language* by David Crystal (Cambridge University Press 1992)

– *Concise Dictionary of English Etymology* by Walter W. Skeat (Wordsworth Reference 1993)

– *Dictionary of Foreign Words And Phrases In Current English* by Alan Bliss (Routledge 1966)

– *History of the English Language* by Albert C. Baugh and Thomas Cable (Routledge 1993)

– *Oxford Dictionary of New Words* by Sara Tulloch (Oxford University Press 1991)

– *Slang Down The Ages* by Jonathan Green (Kyle Cathie 1993)

– *True Etymologies* by Adrian Room (Routledge and Kegan Paul 1988)

– *Concise Oxford Dictionary of English Etymology* by T.F. Hoad (Oxford University Press 1993)

– *Dictionary of Word And Phrase Origins* by Martin Manser (Sphere 1990)

Spotlight on MORPHOLOGY

– Look at the bits inside words. The smallest unit of meaning in a word is a morpheme. There are two kinds: **free morphemes** which can stand alone to make meaning, for example and **bound morphemes** which don't make meaning until they are added on to a free morpheme. The words *sight* and *excite*, for example, are free morphemes. They can each stand alone to make meaning. Bound morphemes can be added to them to form more words:

sight	excite
insight	excited
unsightly	exciting
short-sighted	unexciting
oversight	excitable

We use bound morphemes in English to change nouns to adjectives, adjectives to adverbs. Does it work in the same way in children's home languages?

- Look at mid-word code switching. Bilinguals often pick out morphemes unconsciously when they combine one bit of a word from L_1 with another bit of a word from L_2.

- Compare English-Panjabi word-switches with Franglais.

Spotlight on SYLLABLES

Syllabic segmentation is different from morphology! The words *satis-faction* and *clover* are both single free morphemes. But we can play with the syllables they are composed of in all sorts of ways:

And, wrapping it up...

here is a collection of strategies, activities and resources which teachers and student-teachers have used successfully to build a meaning-seeking ethos in their classrooms.

Display

Stick 'em up! – funny, scary, noisy words – displayed in lots of languages

> **an adjective alligator**
> **a metaphor monster**
> **a word wall**

Graphic Poetry

is a great way to focus on word meanings. Look at verse by Michael Rosen, Roger McGough and others. Use computers to produce graphic representations of meaning ...

SHRINKING and s - t - r - e - t - c - h i n g

Drama, PE and Movement

One student-teacher used dance and movement to explore word-meanings in poetry, then brought the children together in a circle at the end of the lesson. 'Instead of *sad* and *very sad*, the children used words like *heartbroken, frustrated, friendless, shaky, miserable.*' The student concluded that personal projection into the drama role stimulated a greater range of vocabulary and deeper insight into the meanings of the poem.

– Take target words/idioms/proverbs on cards into PE/dance/drama/movement lessons. Spread the words on the floor and work in pairs to interpret them through movement

– Use PE and movement to be a *slithering snake*, then *a perilous python*; *a harassed parent* then *a harassed hedgehog*; *a satisfying meal* then a *satisfactory conclusion...*

The Overhead Projector

Use transparencies for songs and rhymes, children's work, magazine cuttings, jokes...

– Project the transparency onto a whiteboard and ring lexical items using a marker pen

– Make a collection of overhead transparencies in hanging plastic sleeves for children to use

– Use the OHP for whole class/group reading of rhymes and poems:

> Hot cross buns
>
> Hot cross buns
>
> One a penny, two a penny
>
> Hot cross buns
>
> If you have no daughters
>
> Give them to your sons
>
> One a penny, two a penny
>
> Hot cross buns

– Use a Rich Scripting approach to preparing questions:

What's the song about?

What are the buns made of? [ingredients, check packet!]

What do they look like? [shape, colour, glaze, texture, top, bottom, inside]

Who sings the song?

Where are they singing? [street, baker's shop, supermarket]

Who do they sing the song to? [mum, dad, boys and girls]

How are the buns heated? [fire, oven, microwave]

What's the cross? [angry; cross the road; symbolism]

Arc the buns all the same? [big, small, plain, rich]

How do we eat them? [warm sliced, spread butter/marg.]

What do they taste like?

GOOD FRIDAY BREAKFAST – COMPARE RAMADAN AND EID

HAND ACTION GAME

PUPPETS/SHOP

BAKER'S HAT/TONGS/PAPER BAGS

PENNIES – sets; times 2; halves

HOT	}	use dictionaries/thesauri to explore
CROSS	}	multiple meanings, collocations and
BUN	}	cultural connotations of these words

• Make changes to texts on the OHP with groups or a whole class, using thesauri:

Mehnaz had a little lamb Its fleece was white as snow And everywhere that Mehnaz went The lamb was sure to go	Mehnaz had a _____ lamb Its _____ was _____ __ _____ And everywhere that Mehnaz went The lamb was _____ to go
It followed her to school one day Which was against the rules It made the children laugh and shout To see the lamb in school	It _____ her to school one day Which was _____ ___ _____ It made the children _____ and___ To see the _____ in school
And so the teacher turned it out But still it lingered near And waited patiently about Till Mehnaz did appear	And so the teacher _____ __ __ But still it _____ near And waited _____ about Till Mehnaz did _____
'Why does the lamb love Mehnaz so?' The eager children cried; 'Why, Mehnaz loves the lamb, you know' The teacher did reply.	'Why does the lamb love Mehnaz so?' The _____ children cried. 'Why, Mehnaz _____ the lamb, you know' The teacher did _____.

Dictionary Dipping

– at registration time, open your dictionary and read about a word or expression which makes a connection with the day's news or activities

– Children open the dictionary or thesaurus at random and ask you and others about your understanding of words and phrases they find.

Street Talk

– Collect play on words in adverts

– make a collage of street signs

– collect rhyme and alliteration in environmental signs and labels

Feathers, Furs and Fins – pet shop

Posh wash – launderette

Muk Tubs – skip hire

Buttons, Buckles and Bows – haberdashery shop

Jokes

They're serious stuff.

By age seven, children are very keen to join the 'knock knock' and 'doctor doctor' **joke club**. They do not 'get' all the jokes, but the important thing is to nourish their desire to do so. Interlingual jokes will draw on homophones from L$_1$ and English and '*faux amis*' (see Chiario, 1992). English mother-tongue speakers and EAL pupils who are culturally proximate will acquire English jokes and word play on TV – others won't, and some families anyway will restrict viewing or have alternative TV diets.

– Tell a joke to two children in the morning. Tell them it's their job to teach it to everyone in the class before they go home. Don't worry about 'spoiling' the joke!

– Mix up joke questions and answers on card, or on the computer, for children to sort:

How do you get two whales in a mini?	A banana disguised as a cucumber.
Now you see it, now you don't. What is it?	William the Conker.
What can't you do if you put 250 melons in the fridge?	A bulldozer.
What did the big candle say to the little candle?	A hotdog.
What do birds get when they're poorly?	A killer butterfly.
What do you call a 400 kilogram grizzly bear?	A lemon with a loose connection.
What do you call a sleeping bull?	A watchdog.
What does a ball do when it stops rolling?	Because they can't stand the smell of their feet.
What dog has no tail?	Because you might step in a poodle.
What goes ha-ha-ha clonk?	Drive down the motorway. (Two whales = to Wales!)
What goes tick-tick-woof-woof?	Flu.
What is yellow and flickers?	Looks round.
What's pretty, has big teeth and flies?	Moo York
What's yellow on the inside and green on the outside?	Shut the door?
When it's raining cats and dogs, why do you have to be careful?	Sir.
Where do cows go on holiday?	Someone laughing their head off.
Where does a dog go when it loses its tail?	To a retailer.
Which chestnut invaded Britain?	To get to the Bird's Eye shop.
Why did the one-eyed chicken cross the road?	A black cat walking over a zebra crossing
Why do giraffes have long necks?	You're too young to go out at night.

(Thanks to Avril Brock and Barré Fitzpatrick for this awful lot)

Word-Weaving

Word-Weaving is of course a metaphor. EAL learners need actively to engage in semantic exploration in and out of different contexts of curriculum, in and out of literal, figurative, connotative meanings, in and out of different languages and the different cultural milieux of home and school. The metaphor of 'weaving' first took on a physical reality when teachers and children in a Year Five class[1] first began to focus on key lexical items in geography and history and explore their meaning potential. The first step was the 'Rich Scripting' approach to lesson planning by the teachers (see pp 90-91).

After each lesson the children took home a WORD WEAVER CARD to extend their semantic investigation across their home languages. Their task was to find equivalent meanings in home languages for the geography and history words they had been learning.

The home assignment cards aimed to span EAL children's linguistic repertoire by involving families and alerting them to the value of inter-lingual exploration. The information brought back to school on the cards was then transferred to bright strips of paper and placed on a **Word-Weaving loom** – a simple wooden frame that stood on a cupboard-top and which became a focal feature of the classroom. In turn, different children had the task of weaving the loom with the words that the class explored over the course of the topic. *Word-Weaving* thus had concrete reality as well as metaphoric meaning.

WORD WEAVER'S NAME Gurpreet Thandi Majid Bashir

HOME LANGUAGE Punjabi

Date 7.3.96

Target word or phrase in English	box

Words or phrases with the same meaning in home language	Daba : Put things in diffrent merated container, Jack in the box, box jaur ears

Sentences in English and other languages   A fight with fists as a sport.

Sources of information:

	√			√
Family member		Thesaurus		
Friend	✓	Glossary		
Teacher		Encyclopaedia		
English dictionary	✓	TV		
Bilingual dictionary		Other		

WORD WEAVER'S NAME. Sabina Sharat + Nurul Abu Bakar

HOME LANGUAGE. Gugrati + Malay

Date

Target word or phrase in English

top

Words or phrases with the same
meaning in home language

Atas + top (Malay) da kru + top (Gugrati)

Sentences in English and other
languages

TOP of the class

	malay	Gugrati	malay	Gugrati
Spinning top :	gasing	bama do	Kethar	Haru
musical top :	same.	chakardi		
which he were :	bagu	Gangi		
top lid :	Pemutup	dakru		

Sources of information: √ √

Family member	✓	Thesaurus		
Friend		Glossary		
Teacher		Encyclopaedia		
English dictionary		TV		
Bilingual dictionary		Other	✓

WORD WEAVER'S NAME. Julekha Mottura. Nazia Bahadur

HOME LANGUAGE. Gugrati X urda.

Date

Target word or phrase in English

Stand.

Words or phrases with the same
meaning in home language

uth and karah

Sentences in English and other
languages

A book stand. ઊ/uth ા I cannot stand it.
Stand up for someone. karah* ઊ uth ા karah
Stand up. music stand.

Sources of information: √ √

Family member	✓✓	Thesaurus		
Friend	✓	Glossary		
Teacher		Encyclopaedia		
English dictionary		TV		
Bilingual dictionary		Other		

Acknowledgements: thanks to Caroline Charles and children of Waverley Middle School.

The loom turned out to be a highly effective attention-catching device. It has since been used in primary and nursery classrooms, by pairs and groups of children, and for whole-class work.

The motivation of EAL pupils to engage with lexical meanings in ways which enhance their curriculum learning, depends crucially on the classroom ethos engendered by the teacher and on the knowledge about language (KAL) that is applied consciously and analytically in the classroom. The more the links between lexical semantics, pedagogy and other cognitive sciences are clarified, the more KAL becomes accessible as teaching strategies. What seems certain from the children's eager responses to *Word-Weaving* is that their propensity to explore words is waiting to be kindled into a powerful learning tool (see McWilliam 1996 and 1997).

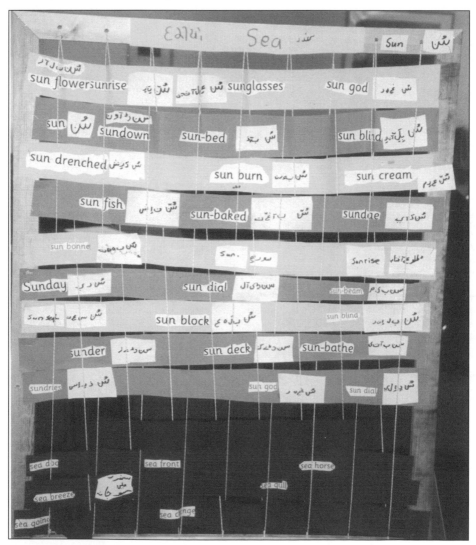

Mistaken meaning may show up in translation! Here, some literal equivalents show the need for more attention to compound words and to translation skills.

Thankyou Maggie Power and children of Grange
Road First School

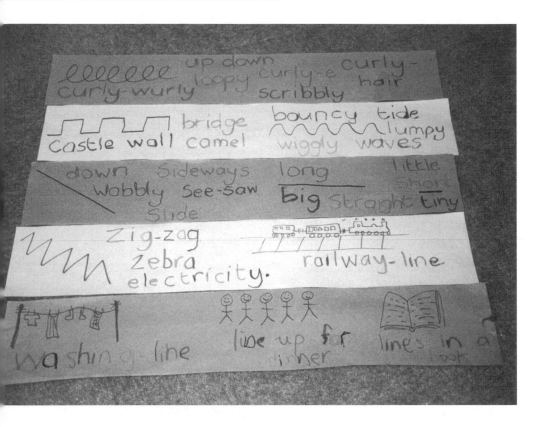

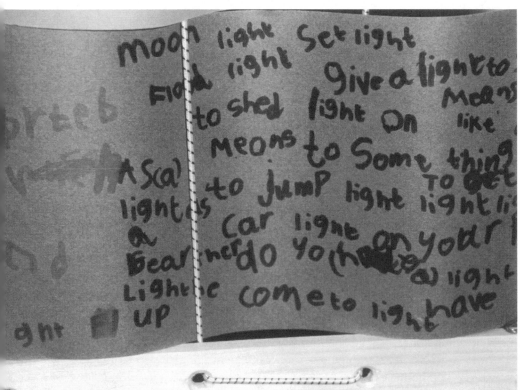

With thanks to teachers participating in the
in-service course 'Word-Weaving' 1996

The loom is intended to be an attention-seeking device for making word-meaning exploration visible and engaging. Writing and pictures on any size or kind of paper can be woven in and out of the elastic strings. Small pieces (for example newspaper cuttings) can be taped or stapled together in strips so that they reach from side to side. Eye-catching effects can be created by bold writing on coloured paper off-cuts and ends of wall-paper, with writing-paper pasted onto strips of luminous paper and silver foil, with print from magazines and product packages, with computer print in large fonts, etc.

Some of the most successful users of the loom were the children themselves. For example, give a small group of children the job of Word-Weavers for a whole day (perhaps equipped with Word-Weaver badges and clipboards). The teacher starts the process off by **modelling** ways of exploring word-meaning – using dictionaries and thesauri, perhaps, or telling a short story (or joke) which features certain words and phrases for the children to focus on.

Word-Weaving can take place as an integral part of curriculum topic work, be a device for collaboration between English/subject teachers (where these are separately timetabled), or it can be a focused activity in its own right for a group or for whole class work. For example, children might pick out a few words from a story and investigate multiple meanings and cultural connotations by asking class-mates and adults about them.

The loom is a working tool for children at any stage of literacy development. With children at early stages, the loom might be filled with emergent writing combined with the teacher's writing or with printed words, phrases and sentences relevant to the day's activities. Older children will be able to fill the loom with the results of exploring perhaps just one word or expression. The use of dictionaries and thesauri varies according to whether the children are able to handle them independently or need teacher input. Even very young children are fascinated when teachers model the use of big adult dictionaries and teachers are frequently surprised at the ideas they have about word-meanings.

As a working tool over which they have control, the loom encourages children to take risks. Errors in spelling, translations and meanings are part of the learning. Teachers who share children's home languages need to view errors in L_1 as developmental and correct them in ways which encourage further attempts. In EAL the same applies. In groups combining EAL and English mother-tongue children the loom brings tacit metalinguistic knowledge into consciousness as they discuss, read and write together.

When the day's Word-Weavers have finished filling the loom – perhaps with their own group's work or with work collected from the whole class, the report-back session includes **shared imaging**, so that the whole class develops the habit of finding out from one another what ideas they have about words, idioms, figurative expressions etc. and the word-meaning consciousness continues when the children go home.

Boning Up...

RESOURCES

A number of valuable resources for classroom activities and teacher reference not so far mentioned are listed below:

– Reader's Digest *Reverse Dictionary*: *how to find the words on the tip of your tongue* (Reader's Digest)

'Instead of starting with a headword and moving on to the definition, as in a conventional dictionary, the Reverse Dictionary starts with the definition... and leads from there to the word you are seeking.' The book has an absorbing collection of entries, including charts and illustrations for categorizations, collocations, synonyms and opposites.

– *Cobuild English Dictionary* + *Workbook* (Harper Collins)

This dictionary is based on words *as they are used* by native speakers of English. Words which have multiple meanings (in collocation) are exemplified and explained and their frequency coded. Natural phraseology is given priority so EAL learners are provided with good models of usage for speaking and writing.

– *Cobuild Dictionary of Idioms* + *Workbook* (Harper Collins)

The introduction explains their usefulness: 'If you do not know that the words [in idioms] have a special meaning together, you may well misinterpret what someone is saying, or be puzzled why they are saying something that is untrue or irrelevant.' A great resource for 'dictionary dipping'.

– *Spelling and Language Skills* by Angela Redfern (Scholastic)

A readily usable collection of photocopiable activities – most designed to develop phonological awareness, but also attending to word-meaning and linguistic diversity.

– *The Languages Book* by Mike Raleigh (English and Media Centre, London or through National Association for the Teaching of English)

A long-standing favourite, this book comes from the 'good old days' of language awareness and you will find it (unwittingly) endorsed by National Curriculum English Programmes of Study, Key Stages 2, 3 and 4.

– *Looking into Language: classroom approaches to knowledge about language* edited by Richard Baines, Bernadette Fitzgerald and Mike Taylor (Hodder and Stoughton)

A product of the Language in the National Curriculum (LINC) project coordinated by Ronald Carter. The collection of case studies here include attention to vocabulary and word-meaning in oracy and literacy.

– *Teaching and Learning Vocabulary* by Linda Taylor (Prentice Hall)

A book intended for teaching English as a 'foreign' language to students world-wide. This is not an approach which sets EAL in the context of curriculum learning but one which I would encourage teachers of older EAL learners to look at, since it takes word-meaning as its focus. Many teaching techniques for EAL and EFL learners are transferable.

– *Looking Up: An Account of the Cobuild project in lexical computing* edited by J.M. Sinclair (Collins)

Explains the process of corpus development and database compilation. Shows how lexicographers are now able to make use of massive computer data-banks to compile dictionaries based on 'real' instances of English in use, rather than on 'definitions'.

– *Learning English: development and diversity* edited by Neil Mercer and Joan Swann (Open University Press)

– *Word Meaning* by Richard Hudson (Routledge)

Takes a 'problem-solving' approach to learning about word-meaning and provides a clearly written introduction to lexical semantics.

– *Learning About Language: Issues for Primary Teachers* by Alison Sealey (Open University Press)

Looks at how children's knowledge about language develops during the primary school years and provides practical suggestions for teaching.

– *Teaching Children to Think* by Robert Fisher (Simon and Schuster Education)

A thought-provoking book which helps to maximise the opportunities of curriculum activities to include:
Facts to investigate; Questions to consider; Problems to be solved;
Concepts to explore; Skills to develop; Learning to review (Fisher, 1990).

Note

1   The Word-Weaving project has been reported in *Multicultural Teaching* Vol. 15 No 1 1996, and in *Language, Culture and Curriculum* Vol. 10 No 1 1997.

Drawing by Georgia Woollard

End word

> ... the 'word' is a shared territory; 'meaning' is an individually negotiated understanding (Halliday 1975).

This book proposes that investigations into the academic performance of EAL learners have neglected word-meaning and suggests how teachers can develop it in their classrooms. Ending her fascinating study of children's acquisition of first language lexicon, Eve Clark (1993) contrasts theoretical descriptions of lexicon which offer *static* models of language, with theories of acquisition which aim to explain *dynamic* properties of language (Clark's italics). She argues that: '... linguistic theories don't translate in any simple way into processing theories'. I wish to avoid making any assumption about translating 'lexical behaviours' into a theory of EAL acquisition. What I do propose is that teacher and learner attention to lexical items, illustrative of the 'behaviours' described by theorists, is a prime requisite for EAL children to achieve well at school.

I have pinned my practical approach to vocabulary development in multilingual classrooms on a collection of lexical behaviours drawn from established and authoritative descriptions of theoretical semantics and L_1 child language development. These lexical behaviours highlight the multiple meaning potential of words and phrases (polysemy in collocation, connotation, in homonymy, synonymy etc.), both denotative and figurative, according to their use and interpretation in context (as lexical units). In doing so I have aimed to make links between a number of ideas:

- analysis and targeting of lexical demands in curriculum topics
- promotion of EAL pupils' *semantic agility* across different curriculum contexts
- promotion of L_1 lexicon (with literacy) as the foundation of cultural identity
- atunement to developmental stages of L_2 lexicon and conceptual maturity
- cultural dimensions of word-meaning
- classroom management strategies for negotiation of word meaning
- use of lexicographic resources by teachers and pupils
- 'foreign language' teaching methodologies
- professional collaboration in developing a meaning-seeking classroom ethos.

I have described *Rich Scripting* planning strategies and *Spotlight* sessions as two over-all approaches to foregrounding word-meaning in the classroom. These approaches are intended to provide a framework, not a formula, for developing teacher and learner consciousness of the ways that words behave to represent meaning. By focusing on lexical units – the 'content' words which provide opportunities for learners and teachers to share mental images – I have built on the natural human propensity to wonder about, find enjoyment in, and seek command of word-meaning. This human instinct provides a common bond between teachers and learners and a bedrock of successful pedagogy in multi-lingual classrooms.

The *Rich Scripting* framework gives priority to English vocabulary extension but is much more. It is a strategic lexicographic and discoursal approach which extends beyond the immediate demands of any single curriculum activity. The *Spotlight* sessions are intended to activate children's metalinguistic consciousness, enhance belonging to English lexicon, and reinforce cultural identity by systematically, not tokenistically, attending to home language lexicon. In family interaction, in the street, on TV, in many everyday contexts, words in L_1 and English provide resources for alerting children to the way meanings are represented and controlled. The use of lexicographic resources is particularly effective when children are taught to use adult 'corpus' based EFL dictionaries and when teachers model their use in their planning and manage-ment of classroom activities.

Learning vocabulary entails learning word meanings and it is a life-long process which is rarely, if ever, confined to one language. We are all actually and potentially multilingual and we all possess the instinct to inquire into language and languages in ways which enhance our professional and personal lives. Both teachers who do (in whatever measure) and teachers who do not share children's mother-tongues can make classroom discourse *cognitively* multilingual to the benefit of all. In this book I have limited examples of lexical behaviour to English for two reasons: because English is the target language in which we aim to develop children's full academic proficiency for school learning; and because the examples provide all teachers, whatever their linguistic repertoire, with a lively collection of 'starters' to trigger research for equivalents in other languages, whether or not we know those languages.

Teachers are pre-eminently model meaning-seekers. Teachers are also powerful forces in children's cultural personae. By managing classroom discourse in culturally inclusive ways we encourage children to actively seek meaning in their lives. If we are to succeed, learners must belong. Benevolent tolerance of L_1 in the classroom is pedagogically insufficient; full academic achievement for bilingual children depends on pro-active use of their bilingual resources. I have juggled with age-appropriate ideas, confident in the versatility of teachers to adapt according to their knowledge of children in their classrooms, but I wish to make a strong final plea for high expectations. The most striking aspect of feed-back from teachers who have tried and contributed the ideas in this book is surprise at children's enthusiasm and capability in exploring word meaning, and this includes children of all ages. Expect a lot to happen when you try this stuff!

There are far-reaching curricular implications for meeting the needs of learners in UK multilingual classrooms and this includes many under-achieving English mother-tongue children as well as EAL pupils. I finish writing this at a time when the new mood of optimism in education at a change of government is tempered by gloom at the apparent retention of curriculum dogma. Two watchdogs of education policy – NALDIC[1] and the journal, *Multicultural Teaching* (1997)[2] document the suppression, under the last government, of much needed UK research into teaching and learning issues which have bearing on racial equality and the linguistic needs of ethnic minority pupils. The initial rhetoric of the new government makes little mention of such issues. Whilst other countries such as Canada, US and Australia (see for example Collier, 1995) have invested serious energy into understanding the needs of multilingual inner-city schools, the UK seems intent on bashing on with a content-heavy curriculum strongly at odds with the need to provide more lesson time and vital teacher expertise for classroom attention to linguistic meaning. The alarming consequences of this policy are beginning to show in our schools (see Gillborn and Gipps, 1996) and on our streets.

I am advocating a lexical approach to syllabus delivery – but *not* a return to mechanistic 'word-building' exercises. I propose that we commit professional skills development, curriculum time and resources to our collective multilingual future by drawing on children's own cultural and linguistic resources and by employing coordinated strategies across all curriculum areas.

Difficult *adj.* 1. Not easy; requiring effort or labour; troublesome, hard, puzzling.

Impossible *adj.* 1. Not possible; that cannot be done, exist or come into being; that cannot be in existing or specified circumstances.

Attainment *n.* 1. The action or process of attaining, reaching, or acquiring by effort. 2. That which is attained; esp. a personal accomplishment.

Shorter Oxford English Dictionary 1983

Notes and References
1   details in bibliography
2   details in bibliography

Appendix

Developing a 'meaning-seeking' ethos in the classroom
(findings from the *Word-Weaving* pilot project)

Effective teacher strategies:

- regular use of devices for keeping the target words in focus

- giving clear indications to children that the target units 'belong' in subject domains

- frequent requests for definitions, analogies, multiple meaning (including figurative), appeal to pupils' own experience and home languages

- welcoming responses, with repair and correction, repetition and modelling

- allowing for 'delayed comeback' from more reticent pupils

- humour and play on words

- non-verbal strategies, including mime

- shared 'imaging' in checking on common construction of meanings

- presenting self as model 'meaning-seeker', by using dictionaries in class-room *with* the children, by providing children with evidence of pre-lesson research (including rich scripting), by communicating own enthusiasm for words

- adopting a style of questioning and response which encourages risk-taking

- not assuming that own repetition of the target lexical items 'does the job'.

Children's responses indicate:

- high level and sustained interest by participating pupils in oral word-meaning exploration

- different distribution of boy/girl talk

- high level and sustained interest in 'grown-up' dictionaries [selected from the Longman series] in preference to 'simple/school' dictionaries

- differing understanding of polysemy

- differing understanding of synonymy

- differing understanding of collocational meaning

- differing understanding of superordination (implications for classification skills, need for graphic mapping)

- awareness/ lack of awareness of morphology/root meaning

- awareness/ lack of awareness of homophones/homographs

- awareness/ lack of awareness/ oversimplified understanding of antonyms

- willingness/unwillingness to take risks

- differing levels of competence in using dictionaries/thesauri, including familiarity with alphabetical order (need for structured exercises/visual aids)

- differing understanding of, and facility in, 'translating' and L_1 'matching'.

Scope for extension:
- Collaboration of English/subject teachers (where these are separately time-tabled)

- Building on positive responses of parents to word-meaning exploration across languages and to use of dictionary resources.

'Answers' from pages 9 and 10:

– Humpty Dumpty...

– Jack and Jill..

Bibliography

Aitchison, J (1987) *Words in the Mind* Oxford: Blackwell.

Ashton-Warner, S 1963 *Teacher* London: Penguin

Bain, R, Fitzgerald, B and Taylor, M (1992) *Looking Into Language: Classroom Approaches to Knowledge About Language* Sevenoaks:Hodder and Stoughton

Baker, C (1993) *Foundations of Bilingual Education and Bilingualism* Clevedon: Multilingual Matters

Bialystock, E (1990) 'Achieving Proficiency in a Second Language' in R. Philipson et al. (eds) *Foreign/Second Language Pedagogy Research* Clevedon: Multilingual Matters

Bialystok, E (1991) *Language Processing In Bilingual Children* Cambridge,UK: Cambridge University Press 1991

Byram, M (1992) *Foreign Language Teaching for European Citizenship* Language Learning Journal, September.

Carter, R (1987) *Vocabulary: Applied Linguistic Perspectives* London: Routledge

Carter, R (ed) (1990) *Knowledge About Language and the Curriculum: the LINC Reader* Sevenoakes:Hodder and Stoughton

Chiaro, D (1992) *The Language of Jokes: Analysing Verbal Play* London: Routledge

Clark, E V (1993) *The Lexicon in Acquisition* Cambridge: Cambridge University Press

Collier, V P (1987) *Age and Rate of Acquisition of Second Language For Academic Purposes* TESOL Quarterly vol. 21, 617-641

Collier, V P (1988) *The Effect of Age on Second Language Acquisition for School* Washington DC: National Clearinghouse for Bilingual Education

Conteh, J, Brock, A, Fitzpatrick, F, Power, M and Smith, N (1995) *Classroom Language: the Gateway to Educational Achievement. An Exploration of Connotative and Figurative Meaning in Classroom Discourse* Unpublished research report, Department of Teaching Studies, Bradford and Ilkley Community College

Cooke, J and Williams, D (1985) *Working With Children's Language* Bicester, UK: Winslow Press

Cox, B (1989) *National Curriculum Working Group for English Report, English for ages 5-16* London:DfE

Cox, B (1995) *Cox on the Battle for the English Curriculum* London: Hodder and Stoughton

Cruse, D A (1986) *Lexical Semantics* Cambridge: Cambridge University Press

Cummins J (1986) *The Influence of Bilingualism on Cognitive Growth Working Papers* in Bilingualism No.9, April

Cummins, J (1984) *Bilingualism and Special Education: Issues in Assessment and Pedagogy* Clevedon, UK: Multilingual Matters

Cummins, J (1996) *Negotiating Identities: Education for Empowerment in a Diverse Society* Ontario CA: California Association for Bilingual Education (distributed in UK by Trentham Books)

d'Antin Van Rooten, L (1977 edition) *Mots d'Heures: Gousses, Rames, The d'Atin Manuscript* Brighton: Angus and Robertson

DES (1988) *Report of the Committee of Inquiry into the Teaching of English Language [Kingman Report]* London: HMSO

DES and the Welsh Office (1989) *English for Ages 5-16 [The Cox Report]* London: HMSO

DfEE *National Curriculum Key Stages 1and2* 1995 London: Department for Education

Donaldson, M (1978) *Children's Minds* London: Fontana

Education Department, Western Australia (1994 / 96) *First Steps* Distributed in UK by Heinemann

Educational Trust, *Educational Trust Pictorial Chart no. 735* available from Educational Trust, 27 Kirchen Road London W13 OUD

Edwards, V (1986) *Language in a Black Community* Clevedon: Multilingual Matters

Ellis, R (1994) *The Study of Second Language Acquisition* Oxford: Oxford University Press

Fisher, R (1990) *Teaching Children to Think* Simon and Schuster

Fisher, S and Hicks, D (1985) *World Studies 8 - 13* Oliver and Boyd

Fitzpatrick, F (1987) *The Open Door: The Bradford Bilingual Project* Clevedon, UK: Multilingual Matters

Fitzpatrick, F (1996) *Unpublished Notes* Department of Teaching Studies, Bradford and Ilkley Community College

Fitzpatrick, F. and McWilliam, N (1995) A Perspective on Teacher Education for Work in Multilingual Classrooms in *Invitational Conference on Teaching and Learning English as an Additional Language: Conference Papers* London, UK: SCAA Publications.

Gibbons, P (1991) *Learning To Learn In A Second Language* NSW, Aust.: Primary English Teaching Association (distributed in UK by Madaleine Lindley Books Ltd., Oldham)

Gillborn, D and Gipps, C (1996) *Recent Research on the Achievement of Ethnic Minority Pupils* London: HMSO

Graddol, D, Cheshire, J and Swann, J (1987) *Describing Language* Milton Keynes: Open University Press

Gregory, E (1996) *Making Sense of a New World: Learning to Read in a Second Language* London: Paul Chapman

Haastrup, K (1991) *Lexical Inferencing Procedures or Talking About Words* Tübungen: Gunter Narr Verlag Tübungen

Halliday, M (1975) *Learning How to Mean: Explorations in the Development of Language* London: Edward Arnold

Halliday, M (1978) *Language as a Social Semiotic* London: Edward Arnold

Hammerly, H (1991) *Fluency and Accuracy* Avon, UK: Multilingual Matters

Hardy, G (1997) *Unpublished Masters Dissertation* University of Sheffield

Hudson, R (1995) *Word Meaning* Routledge

Jackendoff, R (1983) Semantics and Cognition Massachussets:MIT Press

Jackson, H (1988) *Words and Their Meanings* London: Longman

Kingman Report: *Committee of Inquiry into the Teaching of English Language* (1988) London: DES

Labov, W (1969) 'The Logic of Non-Standard English' in J. Atlantis (ed) *School of Languages and Linguistics Monograph Series no 22* Washington: Georgetown Press

Lakoff, G (1987) *Women, Fire and Dangerous Things* Chicago: University of Chicago Press

Lakoff, G and Johnson, M (1980) *Metaphors We Live By* Chicago: University of Chicago Press.

Lee, V and Das Gupta, P (1995) *Children's Cognitive and Language Development* Oxford: Blackwell

Leech, G (1974) *Semantics: The Study of Meaning* Harmondsworth, England: Penguin Books

LINC Project Teaching Materials *Language in the National Curriculum* (1991) Withheld from Publication by Minister of State

Lyons, J (1995) *Linguistic Semantics* Cambridge: Cambridge University Press

Malavé, L M and Duquette G (eds) (1991) *Language, Culture and Cognition* Clevedon, UK: Multilingual Matters.

McWilliam, N (1996) 'Word-Weaving: Exploring Meaning in the Multilingual Classroom' in *Multicultural Teaching* Vol. 15 No. 1.

McWilliam, N (1997) 'Lexical Meaning in the Multilingual Classroom: The Word-Weaving Project' in *Language, Culture and Curriculum* Vol. 10, No. 1.

McWilliam, N (in progress) *Learning to Attend to Word-Meaning in Multilingual Primary Classrooms – a study of lexical consciousness in beginning teachers* PhD thesis in progress, University of Bradford

Meara, P (1984) 'The Study of Lexis in Interlanguage' in R. Ellis (ed) (1994) *The Study of Second Language Acquisition* Oxford University Press

Mercer, N and Swann, J (1996) *Learning English: Development and Diversity* Routledge

Multicultural Teaching Journal 1997 vol 15 Number 3 Stoke-on-Trent: Trentham Books

NALDIC National Association of Language Development in The Curriculum

O'Malley, J M and Chamot, A U (1990) *Learning Strategies in Second language Acquisition* Cambridge: Cambridge University Press

Paribakht, T (1985) 'Strategic Competence and Language Proficiency' in *Applied Linguistics,* 6, 132-46

Reynell, J (1980) 'Language Development and Assessment' in J. Cooke and D. Williams (1985) *Working With Children's Language* Bicester, UK: Winslow Press

Richards, I A (1936) *The Philosophy of Rhetoric* Oxford University Press

Richards, J C, Platt, J and Platt, H (1992) *Dictionary of Language Teaching and Applied Linguistics* Harlow,UK:Longman

Room, A (1992) *Brewer's Dictionary of Names: People and Places and Things* Oxford: Helicon

Saville-Troike, M (1984) 'What Really Matters In Second Language Learning For Academic Achievement?' In *TESOL Quarterly* Vol 18 No 2

School Curriculum and Assessment Authority (SCAA) (1996) *Teaching English as an Additional Language: A Framework for Policy* London, UK:SCAA Publications

Schools Curriculum and Assessment Authority (SCAA) (1995) *Invitational Conference on Teaching and Learning English as an Additional Language: Conference Papers* London, UK: SCAA Publications.

Sealey, A (1996) *Learning About Language: Issues for Primary Teachers* Milton Keynes: Open University Press

Sinclair, J M (ed) (1987) *Looking Up: An Account of the COBUILD Project in Lexical Computing* Collins

Stevick, E W (1976) *Memory, Meaning and Method* Boston, Mass.: Heinle and Heinle Publishers

Stevick, E W (1986) *Images and Options in the Language Classroom* Cambridge, UK: Cambridge University Press.

Summers, D *et al.* (eds) (1993) 'Editorial and Introductory Chapters' in *Longman Language Activator* Harlow: Longman

Sutton, C (1992) *Words, Science and Learning* Milton Keynes, UK: Open University Press

Taylor, L (1990) *Teaching and Learning Vocabulary* Prentice Hall

Thomas, W P and Collier, V P (1996) *National Study of School Effectiveness for Language-Minority Students' Long-term Academic Achievement* Cal.:George Mason University

Tough, J (1979) *Talk for Teaching and Learning* London: Ward Lock Educational

Vygotsky, Lev (1934 /1986) *Thought and Language* translated by Alex Kozulin Cambridge, Mass.: MIT Press.

Way, E C (1991) *Knowledge Representation and Metaphor* Dordrecht, NL:Kluwer Academic Publishers

Willes, M J (1983) *Children Into Pupils* Routledge and Keegan Paul

Winner, E (1988) *The Point of Words: Children's Understanding of Metaphor and Irony* Cambridge, Mass.:Harvard University Press

Wong-Fillmore, L and Valdez, C 'Teaching Bilingual Learners' in M.C. Wittrock (ed) *Handbook of Research on Teaching* 3rd edition 1986: 648-685. New York: McMillan.

Index